SPRINTLINE
2002

INCORPORATING
THE EFFECTS OF THE DRAW

GRAHAM WHELDON

ANDREW MOUNT

DAVID RENHAM

Acknowledgments

Thanks to....
Dave Bellingham for his All-Weather input. Check out Dave's weekly column
'King of the Sand' in the *Racing & Football Outlook*, outside the 'proper'
racing season.

Also thanks to Nicki Bowen for all her hard work researching the Irish courses
(look out for an in-depth analysis next year), to Richard Lowther for his quality
proofreading and to Julian Brown and Sam Pentin for pulling everything together.

Published in 2002 by Raceform Ltd
Compton, Newbury, Berkshire, RG20 6NL
Raceform Ltd is a wholly owned subsidiary of MGN Ltd

A catalogue record for this book is available from the British Library.

ISBN 1-901100-94-4

Designed by Sam Pentin
Printed by Bath Press

CONTENTS

Graham Wheldon

After a brief stint in the broadcasting department at Coral's head office, Graham joined *Raceform* in their Weatherbys office in 1990 before, in 1994, moving to Compton as *Raceform Form Book* Deputy Editor and later Editor. He started a column on the subject of the draw in *Raceform On Saturday* upon its launch in July 1998, a few months after his first book, The *Effects of the Draw*, was published. The column earned itself a big-money transfer to *Racing & Football Outlook* in 2001 and will again be a resident there during 2002.

Unfortunately, lack of room means Graham was unable to go into the other draw-related subjects covered in his previous books, but he is happy to e-mail the relevant material to anyone who doesn't own a copy of *The Effects of the Draw* or *Backing the Draw for Profit*. You can contact him at graham@sprintline.co.uk

David Renham

A regular contributor to *In The Know* magazine and SmartSIG, David has written two books on the effects of the draw, *Bias 2000*, and *Bias 2001*. Although both these sold out, an electronic version of the latter is still available from his web site, www.drawn2win.co.uk. This site was initially set up in 2001 to help promote *Bias 2001*, but is now mainly concerned with a statistically-based racing service. David devotes the majority of his racing time to this service. Racing is not his full-time occupation, however; he is Head of Mathematics at a leading Wiltshire prep school. The long holidays are devoted to racing research and attending meetings.

Andrew Mount

Andrew first became interested in racing at University, where he should have spent less time studying form and more time studying for his degree. While working as a database programmer he developed software to help him analyse a horse's career record by breaking it down by distance, going, class, field size, days between runs, etc. He regularly publishes his findings on internet forums, including www.finalfurlongracing.co.uk, www.trftalk.com and www.directracing.com; he has also contributed to *Raceform Update*, *Racing & Football Outlook* and www.gg.com

CHAPTER 1

English and Irish Draw Biases

Rules of racing No.28(v): *The Starter shall call the names of the runners and, for Flat races, assign the horses to the places drawn by lot, all horses taking their place at the start in the order drawn for them. The rider who has drawn No.1 must always be placed on the left (as from behind the stalls) and the other riders must take their places in consecutive numbers from the left.*
Presuming the stands are on the outside of the course, on right-handed courses, low numbers will be towards the stands' rail at the start of the race. On left-handed courses, high numbers will be towards the stands' rail.

This section deals with the effect of the draw at each track (straight-course races only unless specified) and how it varies on different goings. The 'Best Example' races are for 2001 unless shown suffixed by (2000). All race results are those published by *Raceform*, in the Official Form Book and *Raceform Annual for 2002 (2001 Returns).*

ASCOT (R-H)

The draw only really becomes an issue nowadays when the ground is riding good to soft or softer, in which case it seems the higher the better (although high numbers have also looked best on faster going on occasions).

It's not unusual to see the stalls moved to the far side (and sometimes for flip starts to be used) when the ground becomes really bad, when it becomes an advantage to race as hard against the fence as possible.

On the round course, when the going rides soft, runners invariably tack over towards the outside rail down the side of the track, as that part of the course is partially covered by overhanging trees and the ground is definitely at its quickest there. This had seemed common knowledge in the past, but it was interesting to see only five jockeys go wide in the race won by Hannibal Lad last September (they finished first through fifth):

```
5002- ASCOT (R-H) (Soft, Changing To Heavy After Race 4 (3.45))
Sunday September 30th
WEATHER: persistent light rain  WIND:almost nil
5020  BETDAQ STKS SHOWCASE H'CAP (3-Y-O+) (Class B) (12 Rn)
      4:20 (4:22) 1m 4f £40,600.00 (£15,400.00; £7,700.00; £3,500.00; £1,750.00; £1,050.00) Stalls: High
```

form		age-wt	dist	SP	OR	RR	SF
000-	1 Hannibal Lad [15] (4709) WMBrisbourne dwlt: hld up and racd on outer first 3f: stdy prog over 3f out: rdn to ld over 1f out: styd on wl ....GBaker [(3)] 1	5-8-2	---	20/1	89	93	108
6-	2 Dream With Me (FR) [15] (4709) CREgerton racd on outer first 3f: cl up: rdn to chal 2f out: chsd wnr over 1f out: hld fnl f ....KFallon 5	4-8-9	2	10/1	93	94	106
131-	3 Thundering Surf [23] (4579) JRJenkins lw: racd on outer first 3f: t.k.h and hld up: last over 3f out: gd prog to chse ldrs 2f out: styd on one pce after ....RHughes [4x] 3	4-8-10	1	12/1	94	94	106
/11-	4 Saltrio [87] (2759) JHMGosden lw: dwlt: t.k.h and hld up: racd on outer first 3f: effrt 3f out: rdn and nt qckn 2f out: one pce after ....PRobinson 2	3-8-3	1	10/1	95	94	105
211-	5 Harlequin [101] (2336) SirMichaelStoute racd on outer first 3f: trckd ldrs: pushed along over 4f out: rdn and kpt on one pce fnl 3f: n.d ....MHenry 8	3-7-13	½	7/[13]	91	89	105
004-	6 Mana D'Argent (IRE) [8] (4850) MJohnston lw: prom: led over 3f out: hdd & wknd over 1f out RFfrench 9	v4-8-3	1½	14/1	87	83	104
021-	7 Jumaireyah [15] (4712) LMCumani plld hrd: hld up midfield: shkn up and nt qckn over 2f out: no imp ldrs after ....FPFerris [(7) 4x] 11	3-7-3	1¼	7/[21]	86	82+	103
211-	8 Royal Minstrel (IRE) [25] (4529) MHTompkins lw: t.k.h: w ldrs tl wknd 2f out ....JMackay [(3) 4x] 6	4-7-9	2½	9/1	82	73	101
420-	9 Thari (USA) [16] (4697) BHanbury mde most to over 3f out: wknd 2f out ....PatEddery 15	4-9-4	5	25/1	102	86	98
112-	10 Ahraar (USA) [15] (4709) MPTregoning dwlt: sn prom: ev ch on inner 3f out: wknd rapidly 2f out ....WSupple 13	3-8-2	6	4/[12]	94	70	94
140-	11 Zibeline (IRE) [8] (4860) BRMillman hld up rr: effrt on inner 3f out: wknd rapidly 2f out .....RMullen 12	b4-8-1	6	20/1	85	53	90
014-	12 Adelphi Theatre (USA) [23] (4579) RRowe racd on inner thrght: prom tl wknd 4f out: t.o ..TQuinn 16	4-8-4	dist	16/1	88	---	---

```
2m 41.47s ( 7.42) GOING plus 0.825 per fur (S) OWNER John Pugh (GREAT NESS, SHROPSHIRE) BRED D J Simpson
WEIGHT FOR AGE 3 from 4yo+ 8lb
In-focus: Five of the runners raced against the outside rail on the run down to Swinley Bottom.
```

The Royal Meeting, having produced the following results in 2000 – Nuclear Debate (21 of 23), Observatory (9 of 19), Romantic Myth (21 of 20), Caribbean Monarch (28 of 32), Superior Premium (17 of 16), El Gran Papa (15 of 32) and Harmonic Way (28 of 29) – returned a less conclusive batch last season.

Some felt low numbers had enjoyed an edge in the Wokingham (first three drawn 4, 3 and 2 of 30) but the following Windsor Castle was dominated by a smaller group up the far side. Leggy Lou, easily first home of the stands'-side bunch, later trotted up on her return to the course to show how well she'd run.

BEST EXAMPLES	5f-6f110y	7f-1m
Good	4985	4988
Soft	5258	–
Heavy	5018	5019

Quick Draw: At Royal Ascot 2000, runners racing widest out towards the middle (high) fared best, and last season it was a case of the nearer the far rail the better on bad ground. High numbers are best in big fields (20+ runners) on the round course.

Concentrate On: The top six stalls in big-field (16+-runner) good or faster-ground sprints when the stalls are on the stands' side; the top quarter on bad ground, either when there are 16+ runners and the stalls are stands' side, or in any size fields when the stalls are on the far side.

Avoid: Stalls 1-10 in big-field races (22+) on the round course.

AYR (L-H)

Between 1995 and 1997, and in particular for the last two of those years, a high draw proved crucial in both the Gold and Silver Cups, with runners drawn low rarely getting a look in.

1995 GC ROYALE FIGURINE (27 of 29) beat runners drawn 20, 28, 26, 1 and 29.

1995 SC KESTON POND (25 of 28) beat runners drawn 22, 26, 23, 20 and 18.

1996 GC COASTAL BLUFF (28 of 28) beat runners drawn 29, 27, 25, 2 and 20.

1996 SC CRETAN GIFT (27 of 28) beat runners drawn 25, 22, 5, 18 and 26.

1997 GC WILDWOOD FLOWER (24 of 29) beat runners drawn 9, 1, 7, 22 and 5.

1997 SC PERRYSTON VIEW (28 of 28) beat runners drawn 22, 3, 4, 24 and 8.

In 1995, on ground described as good but slightly faster, judged on times taken, the stands' side was dominant by 5l (SC) and 3l (GC). In 1996, on good to firm, the stands' side was best by 1.5l (SC) and 3.5l (GC), while in 1997 on ground as close to good as you'll find, the stands' side was dominant by 3l (SC) and 0.75l (GC). It always used to be thought that on softer surfaces (as seen between 1998-2000), runners drawn middle to low enjoyed the advantage, but not it seems any more, as recently entire fields have converged either towards the stands' rail, or more recently, down the centre:

1998 GC ALWAYS ALIGHT (8 of 29) beat runners drawn 1, 2, 7, 9 and 28.

1998 SC ROYAL RESULT (4 of 29) beat runners drawn 11, 14, 16, 22 and 1.

1999 GC GRANGEVILLE (17 of 28) beat runners drawn 28, 18, 21, 8 and 26.

1999 SC GREY KINGDOM (14 of 29) beat runners drawn 10, 24, 13, 8 and 25.

2000 GC BAHAMIAN PIRATE (7 of 28) beat runners drawn 2, 23, 10, 24 and 28.

2000 SC LADY BOXER (26 of 29) beat runners drawn 20, 27, 9, 23 and 22.

Trends fans will be interested to know that four of the six winners between 1998 and 2000 had run over 7f on their previous start, while another, Grangeville had run and won over that trip two runs previously. Clearly, stamina is all-important when there's cut in the ground.

It's also worth noting that, apart from on the bog that prevailed in 2000, the Gold Cup winner has come from within six stalls of the Silver Cup winner.

Results from last year were rather less conclusive draw-wise (possibly because the course now employs a Briggs boom for watering, rather than pop-up sprinklers, which were presumably responsible for the high bias in the past). On going described as good, good to firm in places, the results were:

2001 GC CONTINENT (22 of 28) beat runners drawn 12, 15, 20, 4 and 28.

2001 SC TAYIF (17 of 27) beat runners drawn 14, 4, 13, 11 and 24.

Two groups formed in each race and there was little between the two flanks on either occasion, the far side coming out about a length better in the Silver Cup, the stands' side emerging a neck successful in the Gold Cup. A watching brief is advised to start with this year, as in truth Ayr sprints do not presently offer a playable bias.

On the round course, low numbers enjoy a decent advantage when the fields are large, and runners who normally race prominently are likely to find a high draw a difficult hurdle to overcome. Bear in mind here that the old 7f chute is no longer used and that the new 7f50y start is on the round course proper.

1760- **AYR (L-H)** (Good To Firm)
Friday June 22nd

2356 AYRSHIRE (S) H'CAP **(0-60)** (3-Y-O+) **(Class G)** (17 Rn)
2:20 (2:25) **1m** £2,233.00 (£638.00; £319.00) Stalls: Low

form			age-wt	dist	SP	OR	RR	SF
402-	1 **Persian Fayre** ⁸ (2125) ABerry mde all: kpt on wl u.p fnl 2f ....JCarroll 2		9-9-11	---	5/2¹	57	**62**	96
060/	2 **Prideway (IRE)**³⁰⁴ (3847) WMBrisbourne hdwy 3f out: chsd wnr 1f out: nvr able to chal DNolan ⁽⁷⁾ 10		5-8-10	1½	20/1	49	**51**	94
330-	3 **Zechariah** ¹⁸ (1862) JLEyre chsd wnr: rdn and btn appr fnl f ....DaleGibson 4		5-8-3	1	9/13	35	**35**	93
026-	4 **Sign Of The Dragon** ⁸ (2126) ISemple hld up: hdwy over 3f out: swtchd lft appr fnl f: kpt on: no imp							
	....JFanning 8		4-9-0 shd		14/1	46	**46**	93
333-	5 **Magic Mill (IRE)**²² (1744) JSGoldie a chsng ldrs: outpcd 2f out: no imp after ....TEDurcan 9		8-9-4	¾	7/12	50	**48**	92
000-	6 **Muffin Man** ²³ (1735) MDIUsher in tch: outpcd and lost pl over 3f out: styd on fnl f ......GBaker ⁽³⁾ 7		4-8-7	1	16/1	42	**38**	91
/60-	7 **Oh No Not Him** ⁹ (2099) WMBrisbourne midfield: sme hdwy 2f out: nvr rch ldrs .MarkFlynn ⁽⁷⁾ 11		b5-7-13	nk	25/1	38	**34**	91
000-	8 **Pretending** ¹⁸ (1843) JDBethell unruly s: hld up: hdwy 3f out: rdn and btn over 1f out SHitchcott ⁽⁷⁾ 6		4-7-10 shd		20/1	35	**31**	91
/60-	9 **Up In Flames (IRE)**¹⁹ (1824) MrsGSRees slwly away: hdwy 2f out: nt clr run and swtchd lft 1f out: n.d							
	....JMcAuley 3		†10-7-13 1¼		25/1	31	**24**	90
264-	10 **Howard's Lad (IRE)**⁴ (2244) ISemple nvr a factor ....VHalliday 17		v4-9-2	½	12/1	48	**40**	89
000-	11 **Philagain** ⁴ (2244) MissLAPerratt prom tl rdn and wknd fnl 2f ....RLappin ᵒʷ¹ 13		4-8-4	1½	20/1	36	**25**	88
000-	12 **Bop** ²³ (1766) KRBurke nvr a factor ....LEnstone ⁽⁷⁾ 16		v¹4-9-4	nd	14/1	57	**46**	87
0/0-	13 **Whenwilliemetharry** ¹⁰ (2051) ABailey hdwy on inner appr st: sn in tch: rdn and wknd over 2f out .							
	....SSanders 5		4-10-0 shd		16/1	60	**48**	87
/00-	14 **Qualitair Survivor** ⁴ (2243) JHetherton in tch tl rdn and wknd 3f out ....IonaWands 15		6-8-0	nk	33/1	32	**20**	87
035-	15 **Aporto** ¹⁴ (1961) DWBarker chsd ldrs tl wknd 2f out: hmpd and eased fnl f ....TWilliams 1		3-8-13	3½	12/1	55	**36**	83
000-	16 **Jepaje** ³⁷ (1371) ABailey a rr ....KHodgson 12		4-8-9	1¼	20/1	41	**19**	82
000-	17 **Birthday Belle** ⁴ (2244) PMonteith plld hrd: a bhd ....NPollard 14		v5-9-2	1¾	50/1	48	**23**	80

1m 40.01s (-2.95) GOING minus 0.450 per fur (F) There was no bid for the winner. OWNER Murray Grubb (COCKERHAM, LANCS) BRED Aramstone Stud Co
WEIGHT FOR AGE 3 from 4yo+ 10lb

Check out the results of the 14 10+-runner 1m races run over the past two years.

	top third	middle third	bottom third
Win %	28.6	21.4	50
Placed %	21.4	31	47.6

Between 1996 and 1999, there were 23 qualifying races.

	top third	middle third	bottom third
Win %	13.1	39.1	47.9
Placed %	29	33.3	37.7

Six-year stats (1996-2001, 37 races):

	top third	middle third	bottom third
Win %	18.9	32.4	48.6
Placed %	26.1	32.4	41.5

- 38% of races were won by horses drawn from one of bottom three stalls, while only 13% of races went to those drawn in one of the top three boxes. Indeed, the highest stall has not produced a winner in the six years under study.

- If, in every race, you'd placed one point on stall 1, you would have made just over 19 points profit (51% profit on turnover).

- If, in every race, you'd permed the bottom two stalls in a one-point reverse forecast, you would have made a profit in excess of 325 points (a 439% profit on turnover).

- Concentrating on handicaps, the winning percentage for the bottom third increases to just over 58%.

Quick Draw: High numbers dominated the Gold and Silver Cups in the late 1990s, but not last year, and it would appear the new watering system has just about eradicated the bias. Low numbers are best at 7f50y and a mile.

Concentrate On: The top six stalls in the Gold and Silver Cups if the ground is riding genuinely firm; the bottom three stalls over 7f50y and a mile in fields of 10 or more unless the ground is soft or heavy.

BALLINROBE (R-H)

The course is an oval of just over a mile and a high draw is a slight advantage in sprints.

BATH (L-H)

Low draws always used to be considered best in sprints, purely because the course turns left, but recently the most popular theory has been that high numbers are favoured because low-drawn runners frequently go too fast and allow them to pounce late. Essentially, both camps are correct, but that doesn't represent a playable bias.

Concentrate On: Low-drawn front-runners in sprints of 13 runners or fewer as long as the race is not over-loaded with pace; hold-up horses drawn in double-figures in big-field (14+-runners) handicap sprints.

BELLEWSTOWN (L-H)

A sharp track approximately 1m1f round, where the ground invariably rides fast. Low numbers are best in sprints.

BEVERLEY (R-H)

High numbers are massively favoured in races over 5f (give preference to the top stall over the second top over the third top and so on) and also on the round course on good to soft or faster ground. And, if anything, the bias should be increased this year following the work that's been carried out to try and make the final furlong ride faster (it should lead to greater success still for front-runners who grab the rail).

In sprints, runners have to negotiate a right-handed jink not long after the start and it seems harder here than at any other course for runners drawn low to get over to the favoured rail. So Beverley has to be of interest to draw followers (as shown by the following 12+-runner 5f handicaps from 2001):

G-f - SIR SANDROVITCH (13 of 19) beat runners drawn 15 and 7.

G-f - PATRICIAN FOX (14 of 15) beat runners drawn 16 and 8.

G-f - POP THE CORK (19 of 17) beat runners drawn 18 and 12.

G-f - MUTASAWWAR (12 of 16) beat runners drawn 16 and 3.

G-f - LEAPING CHARLIE (13 of 17) beat runners drawn 4 (Sotonian, who won next time) and 19.

G-f - TOMMY SMITH (19 of 20) beat runners drawn 15 and 7 (Beyond Calculation, who won next time).

G-f - TIGER FEET (11 of 12) beat runners drawn 12 and 10.

Good - BEYOND THE CLOUDS (16 of 19) beat runners drawn 20 and 19.

Good - MY AMERICAN BEAUTY (20 of 20) beat runners drawn 19 and 1.

2090- **BEVERLEY (R-H)** (Good To Firm)
Tuesday June 26th

2446 EVE RAIL APPRENTICE H'CAP **(0-60)** (3-Y-O+) **(Class F)** (17 Rn)
4:45 (4:46) 5f £2,457.00 (£702.00; £351.00) Stalls: High

form		age-wt dist	SP	OR	RR	SF
003-	1 Pop The Cork ⁵ (2333) RMWhitaker *lw: mde all: rdn over 1f out: kpt on wl* ......HelenGarrett ⁽⁴⁾ 19	4-9-3 ---	3/11	53	57	101
600-	2 Swynford Dream ¹³ (2102) JHetherton *chsd ldrs far side: rdn wl over 1f out: styd on ins last*					
	....ARobertson 18	8-8-13 ½	16/1	45	47	100
200-	3 Miss Fit (IRE)¹⁷ (1999) MrsGSRees *midfield: hdwy 2f out: styd on wl fnl f: nrst fin* .....CPoste ⁽⁴⁾ 12	15-9-7 1¾	16/1	57	54	97
030-	4 Pertemps Fc ¹⁸ (1962) TDEasterby *bhd tl styd on wl appr last: nrst fin* ....NChalmers 11	4-8-10 hd	14/1	42	38	97
011-	5 Tancred Times ¹¹ (2170) DWBarker *lw: chsd ldrs: one pce appr last* ....TCraggs ⁽⁴⁾ 14	6-9-10 ¾	6/13	60	54	95
326-	6 Danakim ⁵ (2333) JRWeymes *racd wd: hdwy and ch over 1f out: sn rdn and one pce ins last*					
	....PMulrennan 1	4-9-12 nk	20/1	58	51	95
000-	7 Sulu (IRE)²⁵ (1761) MWEasterby *chsd ldrs far side: rdn 2f out: kpt on same pce* ....SHitchcott 20	b¹5-9-7 3½	11/2²	53	35	89
100-	8 Seven Springs (IRE)¹¹ (2170) RHollinshead *prom: irdden along 1/2-way: wknd wl over 1f out*					
	....StephanieHollinshead 13	5-8-8 hd	14/1	40	21	89
002-	9 Dazzling Quintet ¹³ (2095) CSmith *lw: cl up: rdn wl over 1f out: grad wknd* ....CarrieJessop 17	v5-8-11 1¼	8/1	43	20	87
022-	10 Torrent ⁶ (2322) DWChapman *dwlt: a midfield* ....DawnWatson 15	b6-10-0 ¾	10/1	60	35	86
533-	11 El Dolor (IRE)¹³ (2102) RAFahey *wnt lft s: midfield tl hdwy u.p on inner and nt clr run over 1f out: no ch*					
	after ....BMcHugh ⁽⁴⁾ 16	v4-9-9 hd	8/1	59	33+	85
0/0-	12 Scafell ¹² (2137) CSmith *lw: outpcd and bhd tl sme late hdwy* ....MWorrell 4	4-9-10 1	25/1	56	27	84
500-	13 Baby Maybe (USA)⁶ (2214) THCaldwell *a rr* ....BO'Leary 6	b¹3-8-10 nk	33/1	48	18	83
141-	14 Indian Bazaar (IRE)² (2403) JMBradley *cl up: rdn 2f out: sn wknd* ....MSavage ⁽⁴⁾ ⁶ˣ 7	5-9-4 1½	7/1	54	19	81
/00-	15 Lucky Gove ⁶⁰ (981) NTinkler *a rr* ....SuzanneFrance ⁽⁴⁾ 8	5-8-7 shd	33/1	43	8	81
663-	16 Dancing Ridge (IRE)⁶ (2322) ASenior *b.hind: prom: rdn along 1/2-way: sn wknd* ....RLake 10	4-9-2 ¾	20/1	48	10	80
004-	17 Crystal Canyon ¹³ (2095) BSmart *b.hind: s.i.s: a bhd* ....LBranch 2	4-9-2 1¼	16/1	48	6	78

1m 1.50s (-2.70) GOING minus 0.500 per fur (HD) OWNER Country Lane Partnership (SCARCROFT, W YORKS) BRED Hellwood Stud Farm
WEIGHT FOR AGE 3 from 4yo+ 6lb

Runners drawn high on the round course, especially in races over 7f100y and 1m100y, are favoured as the course turns right soon after the start (but don't cross out races at 1m1f207y or further, since racing on the inside rail is a major advantage at every point of the course).

When the going is soft or heavy, there is a strip of ground near the stands' rail that rides significantly quicker than the middle of the course. Under such conditions runners drawn very low hold a decisive advantage (check, though, that flip starts aren't being used – they often are here). The stalls are invariably placed on the far rail, meaning that on soft ground runners drawn low need to tack over to the stands' side in order to find the faster strip of ground (those drawn high tend to stay central).

Here are the statistics from the 44 10+-runner 5f races staged 2000-2001:

	top third	middle third	bottom third
Win %	61.4	34.1	4.5
Placed %	48.5	31.1	20.5

Between 1996 and 1999, there were 72 qualifying races:

	top third	middle third	bottom third
Win %	57	22.2	20.8
Placed %	45.8	31.5	22.7

Six-year stats (1996-2001, 116 races):

	top third	middle third	bottom third
Win %	58.6	26.7	14.7
Placed %	46.8	31.3	21.8

- 42% of races were won by horses drawn in one of the top three stalls. With an average field size of 14.5 runners, assuming there was no bias, statistically one would expect a percentage figure of just under half that (20.5%).
- If, in every race, you'd placed one point on the highest stall, you would have made a 27.5-point profit.
- If, in every race, you'd placed a one-point reverse forecast on the horses drawn in the top two stalls, you would have made a massive 180-point profit (78% profit on turnover).
- Concentrating solely on handicaps (43 races), the top half of the draw has won 39 times (90.6% success-rate).
- The centre of the course here rides somewhere in the region of 5-6 lengths slower, on good to soft or faster ground, than the far rail.

BEST EXAMPLES	5f	7f100y-1m100y
Fast	4235	2092
Good	3937	–

Quick Draw: You have got to be drawn high on fast ground, both over 5f and on the round course, up to 1m100yds (but also at longer distances). On soft ground, everything changes and low numbers are favoured at 5f, and runners who grab the stands' rail are best in round-course races.

Concentrate On: Fast ground - the top four stalls over 5f, the top six stalls over 7f100yds and 1m100yds, the top half at longer distances. Soft ground - the bottom three stalls in 5f races with 10+ runners.

BRIGHTON (L-H)

Low numbers enjoy a definite advantage in sprints when the going is good or faster (particularly front-runners and prominent-racers). But when the ground is soft or heavy, runners often tack over to the stands' rail in the straight, in which case high numbers can hold a slight edge (although jockeyship is often more important than starting position).

Biases tend to become erratic here in the autumn, as the turf seems to get chewed up rather easily in comparison to other courses, and from

September onwards races often boil down to which horse is able to find the freshest strip of ground.

There have been 11 10+-runner 5f races staged in the past two years:

	top third	middle third	bottom third
Win %	9.1	45.4	45.4
Placed %	21.2	45.4	33.3

Between 1996 and 1999, there were 18 qualifying races:

	top third	middle third	bottom third
Win %	16.7	22.2	61.1
Placed %	25.9	35.2	38.9

Six-year stats (1996-2001, 29 races (only three on good to soft or worse ground):

	top third	middle third	bottom third
Win %	13.8	31	55.2
Placed %	24.1	39.1	36.8

- If, in every race, you'd placed one point on the second lowest stall, you would have made a 35-point profit. The third lowest has also have returned a profit.

BEST EXAMPLES	5f-5f213y
Fast	3736

Quick Draw: Low numbers are best in sprints when the ground is good to firm or faster.

Concentrate On: The bottom four stalls in fast-ground sprints, giving preference to front-runners and prominent-racers.

CARLISLE (R-H)

It has long been considered that high numbers are best in sprints, but results from the past five years don't back this theory up, apart from on genuinely firm ground (which is seen fairly often here).

When the going rides soft, low numbers seem to enjoy a distinct advantage, but genuinely soft ground is something of a rarity here, probably because they do not race after August. The new 'gun' watering system has yet to be used, thanks to the course not being able to race last season because of Foot and Mouth.

CATTERICK (L-H)

The first ten planned meetings here last year were cancelled due to Foot and Mouth, with racing not commencing until 7 August, and after that the traditional 5f fast-ground bias was rather turned on its head. Expect

normal service to be resumed this season, though, granted a full campaign.
A basic rule of thumb over the minimum trip has always been that when the ground is good or firmer, horses drawn on the far side (low) hold the edge. However, that wasn't the case in Hout Bay's race last year (4372, good to firm) when the first three were drawn 12, 13 and 17 of 17. When the going is testing, the stands' rail is the place to be, which suits high numbers.

CATTERICK (L-H) (Good To Firm Changing To Good After The 1St Race)
Tuesday August 7th

WEATHER: dull & raining WIND:almost nil
In-focus: This was Catterick's first meeting since February 27, ten fixtures having been cancelled due to foot and mouth.

3695 SAFFIE JOSEPH & SONS H'CAP (0-65) (3-Y-O+) (Class F) (17 Rn)
4:45 (4:46) 5f £2,632.00 (£752.00; £376.00) Stalls: Low

form				age-wt	dist	SP	OR	RR	SF
602-	1 Sotonian (HOL)[21] (3090) PSFelgate prom: r.o u,p to ld ins fnl f ....SHitchcott [7] 13			8-8-9	---	6/12	53	58	97
600-	2 Miss Fit (IRE)[11] (3439) MrsGSRees midfield: hdwy u,p over 1f out: kpt on ins last .....ACulhane 15			t5-9-5	¾	10/1	56	59	95
015-	3 Danakim [7] (3509) JRWeymes mde most tl hdd ins fnl f: no ex ....PMulrennan [7] 4			4-9-1	1	9/1	59	59	94
130-	4 Tancred Times [10] (3453) DWBarker a,p: no ex fnl f ....FLynch 7			6-10-0	1½	13/23	65	60	91
000-	5 Arran Mist [20] (3160) DWBarker bhd: rdn 1/2-way: kpt on fnl f ....KDalgleish [3] 12			3-8-2	½	33/1	45	38	91
201-	6 Marengo [6] (3575) MJPolglase dwlt: towards rr: styd on u,p fr o'r 1f out: nvr able to chal GBaker [3] 10			7-8-10	nk	10/1	50	42	90
/R2-	7 Open Warfare (IRE)[18] (3209) GASwinbank chsd ldrs: no hdwy fnl f ....RLappin 11			3-9-11	½	16/1	65	56	89
660-	8 Adelphi Boy (IRE)[62] (1923) MCChapman sn bhd: kpt on fr over 1f out: n.d .....RStudholme [3] 14			5-9-11	hd	33/1	65	55	89
000-	9 Nifty Major [4] (3612) ABerry n.d ....TEDurcan 16			4-9-10	nk	14/1	61	50	88
602-	10 Strensall [8] (3489) REBarr cl up tl wknd over 1f out ....DeanMcKeown 5			4-9-1	hd	12/1	52	41	88
034-	11 Indian Bazaar (IRE)[26] (2966) JMBradley chsd ldrs tl wknd appr fnl f ....KDarley 9			5-9-2	nk	2/11	53	41	88
040-	12 Susie's Flyer (IRE)[11] (3616) ABerry s.i.s: sn cl up: wknd 2f out ....TWinston 2			4-9-2	1½	11/1	53	36	85
524-	13 Cark [13] (3377) MTodhunter prom tl wknd appr fnl f ....JFanning 6			3-9-7	1	11/1	61	41	84
000-	14 Mount Park (IRE)[21] (3090) DWChapman sn bhd ....DMernagh 17			b4-8-3	nk	50/1	40	19	83
040-	15 Tancred Walk [19] (3178) DWBarker nvr bttr than mid-div ....TWilliams 3			3-8-0	1¼	14/1	40	15	81
400-	16 Dubai Nurse [18] (3209) ARDicken slowly away: a bhd ....JoannaBadger [3] 8			7-7-10	hd	50/1	37	11	81
0/6-	17 Live To Tell [11] (3414) WGMTurner cl up tl wknd 2f out ....DarrenWilliams [5] 1			5-8-11	½	33/1	53	25	80

1m 0.20s (-0.60) GOING minus 0.175 per fur (F) OWNER Tim Dean (GRIMSTON, LEICS) BRED Stal de Kraal
WEIGHT FOR AGE 3 from 4vo+ 3lb

Low numbers are slightly favoured in races run on the round course on good or faster going, particularly so over 5f212y, at which distance runners have to take a left-handed bend into the straight. When the ground is soft, though, horses switched to race on the stands' rail are benefited at all distances (jockeyship then becoming more important than starting position).

BEST EXAMPLES	5f
Soft	5381

Concentrate On: Fast ground – the bottom six stalls over 5f and 5f212y. Soft ground – the top six stalls over 5f and high-drawn horses who race with the pace at longer trips; they have first refusal on the stands' rail once into the home straight.

Avoid: Soft ground – the bottom six stalls when 12-14 runners over 5f212y, the bottom eight stalls when 16-18 runners over 7f.

CHEPSTOW (L-H)

Last season saw the re-emergence of Chepstow as a bias course, after they'd finally kicked off again, following Foot and Mouth problems, on 5 July. Indeed, results throughout the year suggested this is now as major a draw course as a Beverley or a Chester.

At all distances up to and including 1m14y, it was an obvious advantage to be drawn high, and above and beyond that to race as hard against the stands' rail as possible. It didn't seem to make any difference what the going was, either:

Firm – WHY ALYS (10 of 20) beat runners drawn 7 and 18 (the first two didn't reappear afterwards and could be useful).

Firm – TARANAKI (12 of 15) beat runners drawn 11 and 3.

Firm – STOLI (20 of 17) beat runners drawn 13 and 11.

G-f – GREAT VIEW (13 of 15) beat runners drawn 9 and 2.

G-f – TEA FOR TEXAS (15 of 19) beat runners drawn 18 and 4.

Good – TIMELESS CHICK (19 of 19) beat runners drawn 8 and 15.

Good – LAW COMMISSION (20 of 20) beat runners drawn 19 and 16.

Good – INDIAN BAZAAR (1 of 19) beat runners drawn 2 and 9.

Good – GENIAL GENIE (17 of 19) beat runners drawn 20 and 11.

Good – THAT'S ALL JAZZ (16 of 20) beat runners drawn 13 and 17.

Good – CASTLEBRIDGE (19 of 19) beat runners drawn 18 and 15.

Soft – COSMOCRAT (18 of 16, the only one to come stands' side) beat runners drawn 1 and 16.

```
2989- CHEPSTOW (L-H) (Good)
Friday July 20th
WEATHER: cloudy WIND:slight across

3204  JACK BROWN BOOKMAKERS TELEPHONE BETTING 08000 521621 H'CAP (0-70) (3-Y-O+) (Class E) (20 Rn)
       3:10 (3:20) 7f 16yds £3,164.00 (£904.00; £452.00) Stalls: High

form                                                                    age-wt dist      SP  OR   RR  SF
600-  1 Thats All Jazz ¹¹ (2861) IAWood hld up in tch: hdwy 2f out: led over 1f out: r.o wl .DKinsella ⁽⁷⁾ 16   3-7-3  ---    20/1  37   39  105
006/  2 Sir Walter (IRE)²⁰ (53) DBurchell w ldr: rdn to ld over 2f out: hdd over 1f out: r.o .......JBramhill 13   8-7-10  ½    33/1  30   31  104
000-  3 Majestic Quest (IRE)¹⁸ (2644) JNeville a.p: ev ch over 1f out: r.o: eased last strides JonjoFowle 17   3-8-10 shd  33/1  51   52  104
U00-  4 Easter Ogil (IRE)²⁰ (1461) IABalding hld up and bhd: hdwy 2f out: r.o wl towards fin NChalmers ⁽⁷⁾ 12  6-9-7 shd  20/1  62   62  104
003-  5 Who Goes There ¹⁸ (2653) TMJones s.s: rdn and hdwy over 2f out: no ex ins fnl f ...PaulEddery 7   5-9-3 1¾   10/1  51   47  102
110/  6 Unchain My Heart ²⁸² (4929) WGMTurner led: rdn and hdd over 2f out: wknd ins fnl f .....................
....................................................................................DarrenWilliams ⁽⁵⁾ 15   5-9-8 2½   7/1³ 61   52  99
404-  7 Dancing Tsar ¹³ (2814) GAButler bhd: rdn over 3f out: swtchd rt over 2f out: hdwy over 1f out: r.o ...
....................................................................................SFinnamore ⁽⁵⁾ 10   3-9-9  nk   7/13 69   59  99
000-  8 Mind The Silver ⁵ (3062) JMBradley s.s: bhd whn hmpd over 2f out: hdwy fnl f: nvr nrr PDobbs ⁽³⁾ 18   b4-8-9  1   10/1  46   34  97
200-  9 Kanz Wood (USA)²³ (2504) WRMuir chsd ldrs: rdn over 2f out: edgd rt and wknd fnl f .......JReid 8   5-10-0  ½   12/1  62   49  97
006- 10 Danzas ² (3151) JMBradley s.s: sn mid-div: rdn over 2f out: no hdwy ...................MSavage ⁽⁷⁾ 6   b7-8-4 2½   9/1   45   26  94
000/ 11 Pertemps Boycott (IRE)²⁵⁸ (5318) WJHaggas prom: rdn over 2f out: wknd over 1f out GBardwell 14   3-7-10 1¼   5/2¹ 37   15  93
/05- 12 Flying Pennant (IRE)¹⁴ (2784) JMBradley w ldrs: rdn over 2f out: wknd over 1f out ABeech ⁽³⁾ 11   b8-8-3 1½  14/1  40   15  91
040- 13 Addition ² (3147) RJHodges hld up mid-div: rdn over 2f out: sn bhd .......................SCarson ⁽³⁾ 3   5-8-8 1½  14/1  45   16  89
000- 14 State Opening ⁹ (2930) MissZCDavison mid-div: rdn over 3f out: sn bhd .........AMcCarthy ⁽³⁾ 4   4-7-7  ½   50/1  30   ---  89
000- 15 Sakamoto ⁷ (3013) IAWood hld up in tch: rdn over 2f out: sn wknd .................DRMcCabe ᵒʷ¹ 2   b¹3-8-0 1¼  33/1  41   9   87
500/ 16 Akalim ²⁹⁹ (4619) LGCottrell t.k.h in tch: wknd over 2f out ............................ADaly 5   8-9-10  4   25/1  58   16  83
0/0- 17 Vicky Scarlett ²⁵ (2427) PAPritchard s.s: a bhd ........................................CAdamson 1   4-7-10  16  100/1 30   ---  64
/00- 18 Mulsanne ⁵ (3041) PAPritchard mid-div: rdn over 3f out: bhd whn bdly hmpd over 2f out: MHenry ᵒʷ² 19   3-7-12  nk  100/1 39   ---  64
413- 19 Solly's Pal ¹⁰¹ (711) PJMakin a in rr: t.o fnl 3f ...............................................SSanders 20   v6-9-4 dist  5/1² 52   ---  ---
335-  U Pleading ²⁷ (2398) MABulleky s.s: swtchd stands' side: bhd whn strnbld and uns rdr o'r 4f out MFenton 9   v8-9-7  ---  7/1³ 55   ---  ---
1m 23.20s ( -0.10) GOING plus 0.125 per fur (G) OWNER John Purcell (UPPER LAMBOURN, BERKS) BRED John Purcell
LONG HANDICAP Vicky Scarlett (GB) 6-12 Mulsanne (GB) 7-3 Sir Walter (IRE) 7-6 Pertemps Boycott (IRE) 7-8
WEIGHT FOR AGE 3 from 4yo+ 7lb
```

The management are apparently planning to use an 'earthquake' machine this season in a bid to break up any ground which has become compacted. If this is a similar machine to the one used by Goodwood to break up the inside rail a few years ago, it could well mean an end to the bias, so a watching brief is advised to start with.

There have been 48 10+-runner straight-course races staged in the past two years:

	top third	middle third	bottom third
Win %	58.3	20.8	20.8
Placed %	44.4	30.6	25

Taking only races from last year, the percentages become even more significant:

	top third	middle third	bottom third
Win %	69.9	8.7	20.8
Placed %	52.2	24.6	23.2

- The two highest stalls produced 34.8% of the winners in 2001.
- The highest stall produced five winners (strike rate 21.7%), and backing the top box in each race would have yielded a profit of 34.5 points (150% profit on turnover).
- If, in every race, you'd placed a one-point reverse forecast on the top two stalls, you would have made a profit of just over 80 points (174% profit on turnover).
- If, in every race, you'd permed the top three stalls in six one-point forecasts, you would have made a 49-point profit.

BEST EXAMPLES	5f16y-6f16y	7f16y-1m14y
Fast	4736	–
Good	–	4675
Soft	–	3739

Quick Draw: If the planned breaking up of the ground next to the stands' rail by machine has an effect, things could well change. However, if this season is going to be a reproduction of last, then high numbers will again enjoy a huge advantage, whatever the ground.

CHESTER (L-H)

Low numbers enjoy a definite advantage, especially at up to 7f122y, where a slow start from a high draw can be virtually impossible to overcome, given the constant turning nature of the course (statistics suggest the bias is stronger at 5f than it is at 6f).

Soft ground seems to accentuate the advantage enjoyed by runners drawn low, until it has been raced on a few times, when a higher draw becomes less of a problem, as the ground on the inside becomes chewed up. Keep an eye on the starter moving the stalls towards the centre in sprints.

There have been 23 10+-runner 5-6f races staged in the two years 2000 to 2001:

	top third	middle third	bottom third
Win %	4.3	43.5	52.2
Placed %	8.7	34.8	56.5

Between 1996 and 1999, there were 33 qualifying races:

	top third	middle third	bottom third
Win %	9.1	39.4	51.5
Placed %	12.1	35.4	52.5

Six-year stats (1996-2001, 56 races):

	top third	middle third	bottom third
Win %	7.1	41.1	51.8
Placed %	10.7	35.1	54.2

- 34% of winners came from one of the two lowest stalls.
- If you'd backed the horses in the bottom two stalls to one-point level-stakes in every race, you would have made a 72-point profit.
- If, in every race, you'd placed a one-point reverse forecast on the bottom two stalls, you would have made an 83-point profit (74% profit on turnover).
- If, in every race, you'd permed stalls 1, 2 and 3 in six one-point forecasts, you would have made a 188-point profit.
- Horses drawn in the bottom half have won over 80% of all races.
- The inside three stalls have been responsible for 52% of the winners, while the inside four boxes have won 72% of races.
- If you'd placed a one-point reverse forecast on stalls 1 and 2 in every race, you would have made a 98-point profit (169% profit on turnover).
- If, in every race, you'd permed stalls 1, 2 and 3 in six one-point forecasts, you would have made a 228-point profit. (131% profit on turnover).
- If, in every race, you'd permed the inside four stalls in 24 one-point tricasts (remembering that the formula for calculating tricast returns doesn't recognise draw biases as prevalent on round courses and thus doesn't chop a percentage off) you would have made a 570-point profit (82% profit on turnover).

BEST EXAMPLES	5f16y-6f18y	7f2y-7f122y
Fast	1912	1909
Good	2996	–

Quick Draw: Low numbers are best, especially in races of up to 7f122yds, and runners drawn high either have to use up early energy to get into position, or drop in behind and risk almost certain traffic problems.

Concentrate On: The bottom six stalls at all distances.

CLONMEL (R-H)

The course is about 1m2f round, but at present they do not stage sprints, only races of 1m2f and 1m4f.

CORK (R-H)

The course is flat and approximately 1m4f round. Redeveloped in 1997, low numbers hold the edge in sprints, but a high draw seems to offer a slight advantage over 7f in big fields.

CURRAGH (R-H)

The course is horseshoe-shaped, with easy turns and is 2m round with an uphill run-in of 3f. Prominent-racers are favoured on the round course.

Few realise just what a bias there is in sprints here (the going doesn't seem to make a difference). The layout seems similar to the Newmarket July Course and, dependent upon on which side of the course they are racing, runners drawn very high or very low can enjoy a huge advantage.

It's often a struggle to find out which half of the course is in use at any given meeting, but when the stalls are placed on the Curragh (stands') side in sprints and there are 17 runners or fewer, stick with runners drawn very low. When there are 18+ runners, concentrate on the top six stalls. Likewise, when the stalls are on the far side, concentrate on the top six.

Take a look at the past six years' results of the 6f Tattersalls Breeders' Stakes:

2001 BELLA CHICA (25 of 29) beat runners drawn 26 and 28 (stalls far side).

2000 BLUE GODDESS (17 of 24) beat runners drawn 23 and 11 (stalls far side).

1999 HALLAND PARK GIRL (25 of 24) beat runners in 22 and 19 (stalls far side).

1998 AMAZING DREAM (9 of 28) beat runners drawn 6 and 5 (stalls stands' side).

1997 ANOTHER FANTASY (27 of 29) beat runners drawn 5 (proved Group class) and 22 (stalls stands' side).

1996 MISS STAMPER (10 of 30) beat runners drawn 14 and 12 (stalls stands' side).

And here are the other sprint results from 2001:

NEWPARK LADY (14 of 17) raced far side on the far-side half.

REPERTORY (7 of 16) raced stands' side on the stands'-side half (the first one home on the far side, Alegranza, has since proven how badly off she was).

SERIOUS PLAY (4 of 15) raced stands' side on the stands'-side half (the first one home of the high numbers, Minashki, won next time).

4348a TATTERSALLS BREEDERS STKS (2-Y-O) (29 Rn)
3:55 (3:57) **6f** £79,032.26 (£30,645.16; £18,548.39; £10,483.87; £3,225.81; £1,612.90)

form		age-wt	dist	SP	OR	RR	SF
101- 1	**Bella Chica (IRE)**[66] (2314) JAGlover *trckd ldrs on far side: 7th 1 1/2f out: qcknd to ld under 1f out: kpt on wl* ....FMBerry 25	2-8-7	---	12/1		90	---
100- 2	**Partytime (IRE)**[35] (3242) RHannon *chsd ldrs on far side: 3rd 2f out: sn rdn to chal: kpt on u.p fnl f* ... .DaneO'Neill 26	2-8-7	1	10/1		87	---
13- 3	**Lord Merlin (IRE)**[65] (2326) DNicholls *prom on far side: led 2f out: sn rdn: hdd under 1f out: kpt on ..* ....FNorton 28	2-8-12	nk	3/1[1]		92	---
4- 4	**Arkaga (IRE)**[28] (3534) KevinPrendergast, Ireland *disp ld on stands side: hdd 2f out: kpt on u.p fnl f* ....DPMcDonogh 2	2-8-12	hd	20/1	90	91	---
5	**Beau Cheval (IRE)**[35] (3344) HRogers, Ireland *cl up on stands side: rdn 2f out: 5th 1f out: kpt on ...* ....EAhern 6	2-8-7	1	12/1		83	---
6	**Fearn Royal (IRE)**[17] (3907) PeterCasey, Ireland *hld up towards rr: hrd rdn 2f out: styd on wl* ....NGMcCullagh 16	2-8-7	¾	33/1		81	---
7	**Gravy Train (IRE)**[45] (3103) KevinPrendergast, Ireland *chsd ldrs on stands side: kpt on u.p fr 1 1/2f out* ....JPMurtagh 7	2-8-12	hd	7/1[3]		86	---
8	**Sandford Park (IRE)**[6] (4143) KevinPrendergast, Ireland *hld up on stands side: kpt on fr 1 1/2f out* ....JJBehan 10	2-8-12	1½	25/1	84	82	---
203- 9	**Ocean Sound (IRE)**[14] (3824) BWHills *chsd ldrs on far side: kpt on one pced fr 2f out* .....MHills 23	b¹2-8-12	hd	10/1		81	---
10	**Jakeal (IRE)**[17] (3905) EdwardLynam, Ireland *chsd ldrs on stands side: rdn and no imp fr 2 1/2f out* ....JAHeffernan 4	2-8-12	1	20/1	92	79	---
51- 11	**Brest (IRE)**[18] (3684) GCBravery *mid-div on far side: kpt on one pced 50/f fr 1 1/2f out* ......TPQueally 22	2-8-7	nk	20/1		73	---
- 03- 12	**Casta Diva (IRE)**[18] (3704) CFWall *mid-div: rdn and no imp 2f out* ....RMullen 18	2-8-7	shd	50/1		73	---
13	**Double Royal (IRE)**[7] (4141) JTGorman, Ireland *chsd ldrs on far rail: rdn 2f out: wknd over 1f out ..* ....CO'Donoghue 30	2-8-12	1	33/1		75	---
132- 14	**Wicked Uncle**[24] (3558) RMBeckett *nvr a factor* ....GDPower 12	2-8-12	nk	20/1		74	---
0- 15	**Woodland Blaze (IRE)**[30] (3393) CGCox *prom on far side: rdn and wknd fr 2f out* CraigWilliams 29	2-8-12	shd	50/1		74	---
4- 16	**Church Cross (IRE)**[7] (4136) DKWeld, Ireland *chsd ldrs early: no imp fr 1/2-way* ...PJSmullen 13	2-8-12	shd	14/1		72	---
17	**Manchester (IRE)**[22] (3789) APO'Brien, Ireland *hld up: no imp fr 2f out* ....MJKinane 15	2-8-12	½	10/1		72	---
14- 18	**Mine Host**[66] (2306) MLWBell *towards rr: rdn 2 1/2f out: no imp* ....MFenton 17	2-8-12	½	6/1[2]		71	---
106- 19	**Illegal (IRE)**[9] (3968) NPLittmoden *nvr a factor* ....TGMcLaughlin 19	2-8-12	nk	33/1		70	---
20	**Bought Direct**[79] (2076) JTGorman, Ireland *nvr a factor* ....KJManning 20	2-8-12	shd	25/1		70	---
204- 21	**Fille D'Argent (IRE)**[43] (2990) MrsPNDutfield *nvr a factor* ....PCosgrave 24	2-8-7	½	33/1		63	---
150- 22	**Just A Carat (IRE)**[21] (3628) RHannon *a bhd* ....WJSmith 14	‡2-8-7	1	20/1		61	---
614- 23	**Tigress (IRE)**[54] (2654) BJMeehan *led and disp on stands rail: hdd & wknd over 2f out* .PJScallan 1	2-8-7	½	33/1		59	---
24	**Desperado (IRE)**[94] (1889) JTGorman, Ireland *a bhd* ....WMLordan 27	2-8-12	nk	33/1		64	---
25	**Countess Marengo (IRE)**[6] (4143) LiamBrowne, Ireland *nvr a factor* ....TMHoulihan 21	b¹2-8-7	½	66/1		57	---
26	**Cool Ballerina (IRE)**[8] (4133) DKWeld, Ireland *a bhd* ....PShanahan 8	2-8-7	2½	33/1	70	51	---
27	**King Of The Skies (IRE)**[13] (3921) PatrickJFlynn, Ireland *chsd ldrs on stands side: rdn and wknd fr 1/2-way* ....DMGrant 3	2-8-12	3½	20/1		46	---
412- 28	**Sighting (IRE)**[8] (4011) RFJohnsonHoughton *a bhd* ....SCarson 5	b2-8-12	½	33/1		45	---
29	**Libras Child (IRE)**[8] (3351) PDelaney, Ireland *a bhd: virtually p.u and completely t.o* TPO'Shea 9	‡2-8-12	dist	33/1	68	---	---

1m 14.50s (GY) OWNER Carlton Partnership (CARBURTON, NOTTS) BRED W Maxwell Ervine

Quick Draw: The bias in sprints depends entirely upon on which side of the track they are racing. When they are racing on the far-side half, the ground on the far side offers the advantage, favouring high numbers; when they are racing on the stands' side, the stands' rail seems best, favouring low numbers.

Concentrate On: The bottom six stalls in sprints when they're racing on the stands'-side half and there are 17 runners or fewer; the top six stalls when they're racing on the stands'-side half and there are 18+ runners; the top six stalls when they're racing on the far side and there are 16+ runners.

DONCASTER (L-H)

Ultimately there doesn't seem a great deal between the two sides on fast ground (with the exception of early results from 2000, when the stands' rail was clearly faster), but there has been of late on good to soft or worse, with runners drawn centrally having a poor record.

Check out these good to soft or softer ground big-field results from 2001:

SHUFFLING KID (21 of 22, 5f, soft) raced stands' side – only a couple went far rail, this being a juvenile debutant race.

PURE COINCIDENCE (14 of 17, 5f, soft) raced stands' side – nothing raced far side.

GRYFFINDOR (19 of 18, 1m, soft) raced stands' side – nothing raced far side.

MELODIAN (3 of 22, 1m, soft) raced stands' side in the end (drifted over) in a race that offered little guide to any draw bias, the field converging.

CADEAUX CHER (18 of 22, 6f, soft) raced stands' side – nothing raced far side.

NIMELLO (1 of 23, 1m, soft) raced far side – beat the stands' side by 13.5l.

ANNIE'S SONG (1 of 22, 7f, soft) raced far side – beat the stands' side by 4.25l.

KING HARSON (21 of 21, 6f, heavy) raced stands' side – nothing raced far side.

ONLYTIME WILL TELL (18 of 19, 7f, heavy) raced stands' side – beat the far side 15l.

FIRST MAITE (1 of 24, 1m, soft) raced far side – beat the centre by 0.75l.

BOND BOY (17 of 22, 5f, soft) raced stands' side – beat the far side by 2l.

DECEITFUL (20 of 19, 7f, soft) raced stands' side – beat the far side by 2.75l.

FACE THE LIMELIGHT (7 of 21, 1m, soft) raced far side (and was always the furthest over) – beat the stands' side by 1l.

4708- **DONCASTER** (L-H) (Heavy; Races 6 & 7 Were Abandoned Due To Saturated State Of The Track)
Friday October 26th
WEATHER: persistent rain first five WIND:almost nil

5490 AUTUMN APPRENTICE H'CAP (0-80) (3-Y-O) (Class E) (19 Rn)
4:55 (4:56) 7f £3,276.00 (£936.00; £468.00) Stalls: High

form		age-wt	dist	SP	OR	RR	SF
013-	1 **Onlytime Will Tell** 8 (5352) DNicholls *racd stands' side: w ldrs: led overall over 4f out: clr over 1f out: hld on towards fin* ....IMongan 18	3-9-4	---	8/13	73	79	99
222-	2 **Egypt** 18 (5171) SirMarkPrescott *lw: mid-div: sn pushed along: hdwy over 2f out: styd on wl ins last* ... MWorrell (5) 11	3-8-9	nk	11/41	69	74	98
002-	3 **Markusha** 6 (5398) MrsJRRamsden *chsd ldrs: styd on same pce appr fnl f* ....PHanagan 10	3-8-2	5	9/1	57	51	92
000-	4 **Celerity (IRE)** 2 (5447) MJPolglase *w ldrs stands' side: one pce fnl 2f* ....GSparkes (3) ow1 17	3-7-8	4	33/1	52	37	88
546-	5 **Dixie's Darts** 64 (4182) MHTompkins *w ldrs far side: wknd fnl 2f* ....ABeech 1	3-8-7	6	16/1	62	33	81
200-	6 **Xaloc Bay (IRE)** 10 (5287) KRBurke *hld up in mid-div: kpt on fnl 2f: nvr nr to chal* ....PMQuinn 13	v3-8-2	1¾	25/1	57	24	79
600-	7 **Classy Act** 7 (5375) ABerry *sn bhd: sme hdwy 2f out: nvr nr to chal* ....PBradley (3) 16	b3-8-4	1	33/1	62	27	78
/65-	8 **Quinta Lad** 7 (5375) JBalding *chsd ldrs stands' side: outpcd fnl 2f* ....GGibbons 20	3-8-3	nk	12/1	58	22	78
010-	9 **Countrywide Star (IRE)** 21 (5129) KRBurke *chsd ldrs: efft over 2f out: sn wl outpcd* DarrenWilliams 8	3-9-2	2½	20/1	71	29	75
064-	10 **Forest Tune (IRE)** 18 (5171) BHanbury *w ldrs: swtchd rt 4f out to r stands' side: wknd fnl 2f* ...... LPKeniry (5) 9	b¹3-8-6	¾	12/1	66	23	74
400-	11 **Beanboy** 36 (4800) MrsSLamyman *racd keenly: led towards fin* ....NMackay (7) 4	3-7-3	nk	12/1	58	7	73
261-	12 **Baratheastar** 7 (5375) CEBrittain *s.i.s: hdwy on wd outside to chse ldrs 1/2-way: wknd over 2f out* ... RLake (5) 6x 3	3-9-0	2	8/13	74	25	71
010-	13 **Snow Bunting** 7 (5375) JeddO'Keeffe *s.i.s: nvr on terms* ....FPFerris (3) 19	3-8-2	3	12/1	60	4	68
130-	14 **Uhoomagoo** 13 (5267) KARyan *rrd s: sme hdwy over 2f out: sn lost pl* ....DKinsella 14	3-9-4	3	16/1	76	14	64
321-	15 **Flying Tackle** 7 (5374) JSWainwright *w ldrs towards far side tl wknd over 2f out* ....JMackay 6x 2	v3-7-12	2	7/12	53	---	62
000-	16 **Pharaoh Hatshepsut (IRE)** 10 (5287) RAFahey *racd stands' side: chsd ldrs: hrd rdn and lost pl over 2f out* ....CHaddon (5) 15	3-7-5	3½	20/1	51	---	58
454-	17 **Colour Sergeant (USA)** 56 (4402) DonEnricoIncisa *chsd ldrs far side tl lost pl 2f out* KristinStubbs (5) 7	3-7-5	2½	20/1	51	---	55
305-	18 **Face D Facts** 14 (5254) CFWall *s.i.s: sme hdwy over 2f out: sn wknd and eased* ....DMcGaffin 12	3-9-1	4	12/1	70	---	51
000-	19 **Annie's Song** 160 (1452) MrsHDalton *w ldrs far side: edgd rt and lost pl 3f out: sn bhd and eased* ... SHitchcott (5) 6	3-8-5	20	20/1	65	---	28

1m 35.47s (7.81) GOING plus 1.100 per fur (S) OWNER J Hair & D Faulkner (SESSAY, N YORKS) BRED L C And Mrs A E Sigsworth
LONG HANDICAP Beanboy (GB) 6-13 Celerity (IRE) 7-5 Colour Sergeant (USA) 7-6 Pharaoh Hatshepsut (IRE) 7-9

BEST EXAMPLES	5f-6f	7f-1m
Soft	518	523

Quick Draw: Low numbers are best in big fields on the round course.

Concentrate On: The top six stalls over 5f and 6f if the going is good to soft or softer and there are 18+ runners; the bottom six stalls in the Spring Mile and Lincoln if the going is soft or heavy.

Avoid: The middle third in the draw whatever the ground; the top six stalls when 14+ runners over the round mile, the top eight stalls when 18+ runners.

DOWNPATRICK (R-H)

An undulating, tight track 1m3f round with an uphill finish, the course doesn't stage sprints; the shortest distance they race at on the Flat is 1m3f.

DOWN ROYAL (R-H)

The course is sharp and about 1m7f round. High numbers seem to enjoy a definite advantage in 12+-runner 7f handicaps.

DUNDALK (L-H)

The course is undulating and about 1m2f round. The shortest distance at which they race is 7f110y, and there seems no appreciable bias.

EPSOM (L-H)

Horses drawn low in round-course races are able to take the shortest route round Tattenham Corner, and on faster ground have a decisive edge over 6f, 7f and 1m114y, particularly so front-runners and prominent-racers. When the going is good to soft or worse, though, jockeys invariably tack over to the stands' side to look for the better ground.

Over 5f, the stalls are always placed on the stands' side, so when the going is soft the majority of the runners are on the best ground from the outset. High numbers used to hold quite an advantage whatever the ground, but the bias is not so great these days. Certainly, there didn't seem to be a great deal in it last season, the first year the course had employed a Briggs boom in the home straight, rather than towlines.

There have been 12 10+-runner 1m114y races staged in the two years 2000-2001:

	top third	middle third	bottom third
Win %	16.7	16.7	66.7
Placed %	30.5	27.8	41.7

Between 1996 and 1999, there were 23 qualifying races:

	top third	middle third	bottom third
Win %	30.4	17.4	52.2
Placed %	23.2	30.4	46.4

Six-year stats (1996-2001, 56 races):

	top third	middle third	bottom third
Win %	25.7	17.1	57.1
Placed %	24.8	30.5	44.7

- 51.4% of qualifying races were won by horses drawn in one of the bottom three stalls. With an average field size of 12.5 runners, assuming there was no bias, statistically one would expect a percentage figure of around 24%.

Quick Draw: There isn't much of a bias over 5f these days, but there is at 6f, 7f and 1m114y, with low numbers enjoying the advantage on good or faster going (they usually come to the stands' rail on soft / heavy).

Concentrate On: The bottom six stalls over 6f, 7f and 1m114y (particularly front-runners), except on soft ground.

FAIRYHOUSE (R-H)

The course is about 1m6f round with sharp turns. When the ground is soft, there appears a definite advantage in being drawn high at 7f.

FOLKESTONE (R-H)

Before 1998, Folkestone was never thought of as having much of a draw bias (with the stands' rail, if anything, given preference) but nowadays the far rail offers an obvious advantage whatever the ground (accentuated by soft/heavy going).

Very few jockeys used to venture across to the far side, with the stalls invariably positioned on the stands' rail, but as last season wore on it became a rarity to see anything stay near side (expect the trend to continue this year). Check out the results of all the 10+-runner straight-course races from 2001:

CORTON (7 of 13) made all stands' side (none went far side).

WELENSKA (3 of 12) made all stands' side (none went far side).

NIVERNAIS (6 of 16) tracked leader stands' side; second, third, fourth, fifth all raced far side (winner may prove useful).

BRAINWAVE (12 of 13) tracked leaders far side, six stayed stands' side and were beaten 0.75l+.

SUNLEY SCENT (10 of 14) tracked leaders far side, four stayed stands' side and were beaten 8l+.

ANDY'S ELECTIVE (12 of 14) made all far side, four stayed stands' side and were beaten 23l+.

LISIANSKI (8 of 10) made all far side (none stayed stands' side).

BELLS FOR MARLIN (4 of 11) tracked leader far side (none stayed stands' side).

MIRAFIORI (10 of 11) held up far side (none stayed stands' side).

PORT ST CHARLES (2 of 12) held up far side (none stayed stands' side).

MY ONLY SUNSHINE (14 of 14) made all far side (none stayed stands' side).

SCARROTTOO (14 of 15) chased leaders far side (none stayed stands' side).

FULL SPATE (9 of 11) held up far side (none stayed stands' side).

DONEGAL SHORE (9 of 13) held up far side (none stayed stands' side).

DEFINITE GUEST (9 of 15) held up far side, only two stayed stands' side and were beaten 6l+.

It's interesting to note that five of the above winners made all, so give preference to prominent-racers drawn high, particularly when the horse in question is in the top stall and ridden by a jockey likely to get to the far rail as soon as possible.

Flip starts were seen at the opening meeting last season (heavy) and the more astute jockeys improved their positions before they were let go.

There have been 17 10+-runner 5f and 6f races staged on good to soft or softer ground in the past six years:

	top third	middle third	bottom third
Win %	82.3	5.9	11.8
Placed %	49	17.6	33.3

- Horses from the top two stalls won 47% of the above races; the top four stalls provided 70% of the winners.
- If, in every race, you'd placed one point on the highest stall, you would have made a 16-point profit (94% profit on turnover).
- If, in every race, you'd placed a one-point reverse forecast on the top two stalls, you would have made a 28-point profit (82% profit on turnover).

BEST EXAMPLES	5f-7f
Fast	4016
Good	3870
Soft	890

Quick Draw: A high draw is an advantage whatever the ground (and particularly on soft / heavy, when it's a case of the nearer the far rail the better).

Concentrate On: The top five stalls on good to soft or faster ground, the top three stalls on soft or heavy going; give preference to front-runners.

GALWAY (R-H)

The course is tight with an uphill finish and high numbers seem to have the edge in big fields.

GOODWOOD (R-H) & (L-H)

High numbers are favoured on the round course, particularly over 7f, except in very wet conditions (and on cut-up, late-season ground) when jockeys tend to tack over to the stands' side.

The previously decisive advantage enjoyed by runners drawn by the far rail (high) in the Stewards' Cup seems to have all but disappeared as a result of work to break up the surface by machine on that side in 1999. However, the advice is again to steer clear of those drawn in single figures this season:

1999 – low numbers enjoyed a definite edge.

2000 – high numbers were back on top, the first stands'-rail finisher being 3l down at the line.

2001 – GUINEA HUNTER raced centre to far side, beating the first far-side finisher by a neck and the first one home stands' side by a length.

Whatever the 'intensive turf management on the turn for home' carried out over the winter entailed, it's doubtful whether it will stop high numbers being favoured over 7f and a mile, since this bias has always been down to the tightness of the bend rather than compacted ground.

Note here that last year, the course used a 'fanning out' rail on the home turn (designed to bring the horses wider into the straight) as well as the false rail down the far side, up until the Friday of the Glorious meeting. The management seemed happy with the way it had spread the load and don't be surprised to see a repetition this time.

3580- **GOODWOOD** (R-H) (Good)
Friday August 3rd
WEATHER: overcast WIND:slt across

3597 DAILY TELEGRAPH DISCOVER RACING STKS (HANDICAP) (0-100) (3-Y-O) (Class C) (19 Rn)
2:15 (2:17) 7f £29,250.00 (£9,000.00; £4,500.00; £2,250.00) Stalls: High

form		age-wt dist	SP	OR	RR	SF
130-	1 **Venturer (USA)**[14] (3216) JHMGosden hld up midfield: prog on inner 2f out: squeezed through to ld 1f out: r.o wl ....JPSpencer 16	3-9-1 ---	16/1	90	97	104
123-	2 **Royal Millennium (IRE)**[16] (3155) MRChannon hld up bhd ldrs: effrt grg easily whn nt clr run 2f out: nt clr run again ent fnl f: r.o to take 2nd last 100y ....TQuinn 19	3-9-0 1½	11/2¹	89	93+	102
/01-	3 **Lunar Leo**[27] (2838) SCWilliams b: trckd ldrs: rdn and effrt 2f out: styd on one pce fr over 1f out ....MartinDwyer 5	¹3-8-13 1¼	16/1	88	89	100
100-	4 **Lapwing (IRE)**[27] (2838) BWHills prom: rdn to ld briefly jst over 1f out: wknd ins fnl f ....MHills 13	3-9-1 ¾	14/1	90	89	100
135-	5 **Polar Kingdom**[24] (2885) JNoseda lw: hld up wl in rr: plenty to do whn effrt over 2f out: drvn and kpt on wl fnl 2f: nt rch ldrs ....PatEddery 11	3-8-12 shd	10/1³	87	86	99
216-	6 **Forever Times**[27] (2838) TDEasterby hld up wl in rr: pushed along 3f out: prog on outer fnl 2f: nrst fin ....PaulEddery 6	3-8-7 1	25/1	82	78	98
401-	7 **Putra Pekan**[13] (3252) MAJarvis hld up wl in rr: no prog 3f out: hdwy fnl f: n.d ....PRobinson 8	b3-9-7 3½	10/1³	96	84	94
612-	8 **Banjo Bay (IRE)**[22] (2970) BAMcmahon s.s: wl in rr tl prog fr 4f out: chsd ldrs 2f out: no imp over 1f out: wknd fnl f ....RHughes 1	3-8-13 nk	10/1³	88	76	94
006-	9 **The Trader (IRE)**[13] (3249) MBlanshard lw: midfield: rdn over 2f out: no imp and btn over 1f out: fdd ....DSweeney 2	3-9-2 1¼	50/1	91	76	92
313-	10 **Macaroon (IRE)**[24] (2885) MLWBell pressed ldr: rdn and ev ch ins fnl 2f: wknd jst over 1f out ....JMackay ⁽³⁾ 14	3-8-5 ½	9/1²	83	67	92
000-	11 **Speedy Gee (IRE)**[15] (1535) MRChannon led to jst over 1f out: wknd rapidly ....SDrowne 17	3-8-12 hd	40/1	87	70	92
156-	12 **Inspector General (IRE)**[13] (3252) PFICole towards rr: rdn 3f out: no prog and btn whn bdly hmpd over 1f out ....JFortune 9	3-9-2 ¾	14/1	91	73	91
/10-	13 **Kai One**[43] (2330) RHannon chsd ldrs tl wknd 2f out ....DaneO'Neill 20	3-8-6 1	9/1²	81	60	90
104-	14 **Give Back Calais (IRE)**[27] (2838) PJMakin wl in rr and sn pushed along: nvr a factor ....AClark 12	b¹3-9-5 hd	16/1	94	73	89
013-	15 **Matoaka (USA)**[24] (2884) SirMichaelStoute lw: trckd ldrs: rdn 3f out: no prog 2f out: eased over 1f out ....KFallon 15	3-9-3 ½	10/1³	92	70	89
005-	16 **Ashlinn (IRE)**[16] (3155) RHannon racd wd first 2f: prom tl wknd 3f out ....JReid 3	b3-8-9 3	40/1	84	55	85
/40-	17 **Game N Gifted**[77] (1410) BJMeehan dwlt: a wl in rr ....BDoyle 10	3-9-3 6	50/1	92	49	79
050-	18 **Final Pursuit (IRE)**[13] (3241) DHaydnJones swtg: chsd ldrs tl wknd over 2f out ....DHolland 7	3-9-1 1½	50/1	90	44	77
335-	19 **Zietunzeen (IRE)**[10] (3315) ABerry swtg: rrd s and rel to r: a t.o ....FNorton 4	3-8-12 19	40/1	87	---	55

1m 27.93s (-0.31) GOING plus 0.075 per fur (G) OWNER Sheikh Mohammed (MANTON, WILTS) BRED Flaxman Holdings Ltd

---

There have been 26 10+-runner 7f races staged in the past two years:

	top third	middle third	bottom third
Win %	61.5	19.2	19.2
Placed %	55.1	30.8	14.1

Between 1996 and 1999, there were 45 qualifying races:

	top third	middle third	bottom third
Win %	53.3	31.1	15.6
Placed %	45.2	33.3	21.5

Six-year stats (1996-2001, 71 races):

	top third	middle third	bottom third
Win %	56.3	26.8	16.9
Placed %	47.9	32.3	19.7

- The top half of the draw has accounted for 74.6% of the winners.
- If, in every race, you'd placed one point on the shortest priced horse from the three highest stalls you would have made a healthy 62.5-point profit (an 88% profit on turnover).
- If, in every race, you'd put the two highest stalls in a one-point reverse forecast, you would have made an amazing 331-point profit (a 233% profit on turnover).
- If, in every race, you'd permed the three highest numbered stalls in six one-point forecasts, you would have made a 322-point profit (92% profit on turnover).

Quick Draw: High numbers are best on the round course, especially over 7f and 1m, when the ground is fast. However, when the going is soft or heavy, jockeys tend to come over to the stands' rail. Give preference to middle to high numbers in the Stewards' Cup if the ground is fast.

Concentrate On: The top six stalls over 7f and a mile in races of 14+ runners when the going is good or faster.

Avoid: All runners drawn in single figures in the Stewards' Cup unless the going is soft.

GOWRAN PARK (R-H)

The course is undulating and about 1m4f round. Low numbers are best over 7f on good or faster ground, but the bias turns full circle in favour of high numbers on softer going.

HAMILTON (R-H)

It is a huge advantage to race near the far rail (inside) in big-field sprints, but while a high draw clearly helps, it's not imperative as it seems easier here than at many other courses to get across from a low berth.

That said, the course tends to stage a number of sprint handicaps confined to apprentices, and they're always more likely to stick to their draws:

4435- **HAMILTON (R-H)** (Good)
Monday September 3rd
WEATHER: overcast WIND:light, half across

4466 HAMILTON PARK APPRENTICE SERIES H'CAP (FINAL ROUND) (0-70) (3-Y-O+) (Class F) (18 Rn)
3:15 (3:19) 5f 4yds £2,954.00 (£844.00; £422.00) Stalls: Low

form		age-wt	dist	SP	OR	RR	SF
050-	1 Tancred Times [10] (4233) DWBarker *mde all far side: r.o gamely fnl f* ....KDalgleish 15	6-10-0	---	6/[12]	64	66	104
043-	2 Flying Tackle [46] (3178) JSWainwright *prom far side: effrt 2f out: edgd lft fnl f: r.o* ....GBaker 16	v3-8-5	¾	14/1	42	42	102
202-	3 Swynford Dream [5] (4372) JHetherton *cl up far side: effrt 2f out: r.o* ....DMcGaffin [3] 14	8-8-10	nk	7/2[1]	49	48	102
000-	4 Northern Svengali (IRE) [11] (4189) TDBarron *dwlt: sn prom far side: rdn 2f out: nt qckn wl ins fnl f .*						
	....LynseyHanna [5] 13	5-9-2 shd		10/1	57	55	102
060-	5 Jacmar (IRE) [13] (4110) MissLAPerratt *bhd far side: hdwy over 1f out: nvr nr* ....AMcCarthy 11	6-7-10	2	16/1	32	24	98
U50-	6 Pacific Place (IRE) [11] (4189) JSGoldie *outpcd far side tl hdwy over 1f out: nvr rchd ldrs* PHanagan 12	4-8-4	1	11/1	40	29	97
633-	7 Bint Royal (IRE) [10] (4233) MissVHaigh *in tch centre tl rdn and one pce fr 2f out* ......LEnstone [5] 9	b3-8-6	1	8/1	48	34	95
046-	8 Viewforth [21] (3880) MissLAPerratt *racd stands side: hung rt after 2f: no imp fr over 1f out* DNolan [5] 3	3-9-7 shd		16/1	63	48+	95
050-	9 Shatin Beauty [28] (3672) MissLAPerratt *racd stands side: hdwy over 1f out: nvr rchd ldrs* PMQuinn 1	4-7-10	½	100/1	32	16	94
005-	10 Christopherssister [24] (3801) NBycroft *sn outpcd centre: n.d* ....GArnolda [7] ows 7	4-7-10 shd		50/1	39	22	94
000-	11 Robin Hood [11] (4189) MissLAPerratt *cl up far side tl wknd over 1f out* ....SHitchcott [5] 17	4-7-12	½	7/1[3]	39	21	93
030-	12 Referendum (IRE) [19] (3948) DNicholls *racd towards stands side: no imp fr 1/2-way* ClareRoche [5] 5	7-9-9	nk	14/1	64	45	93
200-	13 Double Oscar (IRE) [26] (3716) DNicholls *hld up towards stands side: n.d* ....THamilton [5] 4	v8-9-8	¾	20/1	63	41	92
600-	14 Squirrel Nutkin (IRE) [22] (3864) JeddO'Keeffe *sn outpcd far side: nvr on terms* LindseyRutty [7] 18	b3-8-5	nk	20/1	49	26	91
066-	15 Jack To A King [24] (3821) MJPolglase *missed break: hdwy stands side 1/2-way: sn no imp*						
	....JoannaBadger 2	b6-7-11	1	33/1	33	7	90
000-	16 River Blest (IRE) [62] (2662) MrsADuffield *racd centre: n.d* ....PBradley [3] 8	5-8-7	nk	16/1	46	19	89
000-	17 Millsec [21] (3875) RBastiman *unruly bef s: s.v.s: a wl bhd* ....CHaddon [7] 10	4-8-0	10	66/1	43	---	73
530-	18 Heathyards Signet [25] (3752) DMccain *racd centre: struggling fr 1/2-way* ....GGibbons [3] 6	3-8-6	1¼	20/1	46	---	71

1m 1.00s (-0.30) GOING plus 0.050 per fur (G) OWNER D W Barker (SCORTON, N YORKS) BRED W L Barker
LONG HANDICAP Jacmar (IRE) 7-4 Shatin Beauty (GB) 7-5
WEIGHT FOR AGE 3 from 4yo+ 1lb
STEWARDS' ENQUIRY D Nolan caution: used whip down shoulder and in forehand position
OFFICIAL EXPLANATION Robin Hood : trainer said gelding bled from the nose
In-focus: High numbers had a big advantage here with the first six home all starting from double-figure draws.

Over-watering of the far rail was evident last mid-summer (particularly at the first July meeting) when the course managed to turn the bias full circle in favour of runners who raced towards the stands' side.

A high draw is also an advantage in races over 1m65y as there is a tight right-handed loop into the home straight. It is not uncommon for the ground to become too bad for the use of stalls here.

BEST EXAMPLES	5f4y-6f5y
Fast	2097
Soft	3003

Concentrate On: The top half of the draw in big-field (14+-runner) sprints when the ground is good or faster, the top third when it's good to soft or softer.

Avoid: The bottom six stalls in 14+-runners races over 1m65yds on good to soft or softer going.

HAYDOCK (L-H)

Whatever the drainage work carried out in the winter of 2000 involved, it appears to have levelled things out somewhat when the ground becomes testing. Certainly, jockeys no longer made a beeline for the stands' rail in round-course races last year (something they always did in the past).

As for sprints, it now seems low numbers are best in big fields apart from on genuinely fast ground (good to firm bordering on firm) when the stands' rail still offers the best strip.

BEST EXAMPLES	5f-6f
Fast	2753
Soft	5012

Concentrate On: The top four stalls in sprints when the ground is genuinely firm.

Avoid: All those drawn in double-figures in 18+ runner sprints on good to soft or softer ground.

KEMPTON (R-H)

On the separate sprint track, when the stalls are on the stands' side and there are 18 runners or fewer, a low draw is an advantage, particularly when the going is soft or heavy. When the stalls are on the far side and there are 18 runners or fewer, high numbers are clearly favoured.

The confusion begins in races of between 19 and 24 runners, as shown by the following results from the past two seasons:

G-f – MAN OF DISTINCTION (2 of 21) beat runners drawn 6, 11 and 13. The stands' side finished 2.5l clear.

G-f – ANTONIO CANOVA (19 of 20) beat runners drawn 1, 20 and 3. Nothing came stands' side.

Good – CANDLERIGGS (3 of 24) beat runners drawn 1, 6 and 7. The stands' side finished 2.5l ahead.

Good – PRINCE CYRANO (2 of 23) beat runners drawn 4, 1 and 24. The stands' side finished 8l ahead.

Good – RINGMOOR DOWN (20 of 19) beat runners drawn 18, 13 and 14. Nothing came stands' side.

Good – TOROSAY SPRING (5 of 24) beat runners drawn 24, 22 and 18. The stands' side finished 1l ahead.

Soft – RANDOM TASK (2 of 23) beat runners drawn 7, 4 and 5. The stands' side finished 9l ahead.

It would be fair to assume from these results that both flanks are favoured over the centre of the course, but that would be misleading, since on the two occasions that a high-drawn horse has emerged successful, nothing has come to race on the stands' rail. When the fields have split, the stands'-side group has emerged successful every time. This was again the case at this year's two-day Easter fixture, with Snow Shoes (4) and Mitcham (10) both coming stands' side.

3556- KEMPTON (R-H) (Good)
Friday September 7th

WEATHER: fine WIND:mod across

4573 EUROPEAN BREEDERS FUND MAIDEN FILLIES' STKS (2-Y-O) **(Class D)** (19 Rn)
2:10 (2:11) 6f £4,602.00 (£1,416.00; £708.00; £354.00) Stalls: High

form		age-wt	dist	SP	OR	RR	SF
	1 **Ringmoor Down** PJMakin *unf: trckd far side ldrs: effrt to ld over 1f out: rn green in front and pushed out strly* ....SSanders 20	2-8-11	---	16/1		89+	95
	2 **Amber's Bluff** ACStewart *unf: scope: s.s: wl in rr far side gp: pushed along and prog 2f out: str run against far rail fnl f: tk 2nd nr fin* ....RFfrench 18	2-8-11	½	16/1		88+	94
	3 **Island Destiny** GWragg *w'like: bit bkwd: s.s: towards rr far side: prog over 2f out: swtchd lft over 1f out: rdn to chal fnl f: unable qckn* ....DHolland 13	2-8-11	hd	14/1		88+	94
23-	4 **Lady Links** [48] (3242) RHannon *lw: a w far side ldrs: rdn to chal and edgd lft over 1f out: styd on same pce fnl f* ....DaneO'Neill 14	2-8-11	hd	11/4²		87	93
0-	5 **Voucher** [14] (4221) BWHills *trckd far side ldrs: shkn up 2f out: edgd lft and nt qckn over 1f out: btn after* ....RHughes 17	2-8-11	3	7/4¹		79	89
34-	6 **Candid** [76] (2385) BJMeehan *racd far side: led after 2f tl over 1f out: wknd fnl f* ....BDoyle 17	2-8-11	2	16/1		74	87
5-	7 **Shirley Collins** [58] (2947) MLWBell *racd far side: led 2f: styd w ldrs tl wknd 1f out* ....MFenton 19	2-8-11	nk	20/1		73	86
4-	8 **Thumamah (IRE)** [12] (4278) BHanbury *lw: racd centre: led gp 1/2-way: edgd rt over 2f out: shkn up and edgd lft over 1f out: no ch* ....RHills 6	2-8-11	dht	10/1		72	86
00-	8 **Spindara (IRE)** [15] (4177) PFICole *wl in rr far side: pushed along over 2f out: styd on over 1f out: nvr nrr* ....TGMcLaughlin 11	2-8-11	nk	50/1		72	86
	10 **Blushing Queen (IRE)** JNoseda *w'like: bit bkwd: racd centre: rdn to chse ldr over 2f out: no ch* ....LDettori 5	2-8-11	hd	12/1		72	86
60-	11 **Zacchera** [21] (4022) GBBalding *racd far side: midfield: outpcd over 2f out: effrt and kpt on over 1f out: sn no prog* ....SDrowne 12	2-8-11	shd	25/1		71	85
3-	12 **Crossbreeze (USA)** [26] (3852) JHMGosden *b.hind: trckd far side ldrs tl wknd wl over 1f out* JFortune 9	2-8-11	¾	4/1³		69	84
	13 **Broughton Zest** WJMusson *w'like: bit bkwd: racd far side: midfield: rdn and no prog over 2f out* ....LNewton 16	2-8-11	1¼	50/1		66	83
0-	14 **Sweet Briar** [32] (3680) HCandy *racd centre: nvr on terms and no ch* ....JReid 4	2-8-11	3½	25/1		57	78
0-	15 **Theatrical Waltz** [23] (3953) JJSheehan *racd far side: rr: rdn 1/2-way: sn struggling* SFinnamore 10	2-8-11	shd	66/1		56	78
04-	16 **Artists Retreat** [77] (2363) DJSFfrenchDavis *racd far side: towards rr: rdn over 2f out: wknd wl over 1f out* ....NPollard 8	2-8-11	1¾	33/1		52	76
	17 **Sari (USA)** MrsAJPerrett *w'like: racd centre: hmpd s: nvr on terms and no ch* ....WRyan 1	2-8-11	nk	33/1		51	75
000-	18 **Telegram Girl** [16] (4158) JGSmyth-Osborne *wnt lft s: led centre gp to 1/2-way: sn wknd* PaulEddery 3	2-8-11	1¼	66/1		47	74
	19 **Gala Affair** CACyzer *w'like: bit bkwd: racd centre: hmpd s: rn green and a bhd* ....JFanning 2	2-8-11	1¼	40/1		44	72

1m 14.44s (1.14) GOING plus 0.075 per fur (G) OWNER Prof C D Green (OGBOURNE MAISEY, WILTS) BRED Pigeon House Stud

BEST EXAMPLES	5f-6f
Good	4590
Soft	4483 (2000)

Quick Draw: Low numbers are best in sprints when the stalls are on the stands' side and there are 18 or fewer runners, and when the stalls are on the far side and there are 19+ runners. High numbers are best in sprints when the stalls are on the far side, there are 18 runners or fewer and nothing comes to the stands' side.

Concentrate On: Runners drawn 1-6 when there are 19+ runners (1-4 on soft or heavy ground); the top six stalls when there are 18 or fewer runners and the stalls are on the far side (although look for runners in the bottom two stalls under these circumstances that may come over); and the bottom six stalls when there are 18 or fewer runners and the stalls are on the stands' side.

Avoid: Runners drawn 7-14 in sprints.

KILLARNEY (L-H)

The course only stages races of 1m4f and there's no appreciable draw advantage.

LEICESTER (R-H)

After a good few seasons of high numbers holding the advantage, there were signs last backend that the traditional bias towards the stands' rail was showing signs of a re-emergence. Certainly, in the 7f9y race won by Xipe Totec last October, the small group who raced towards the far rail were at an obvious disadvantage, and it seemed the nearer to the stands' side the better. It remains to be seen whether the drainage work carried out up the stands' rail over the winter will enhance this further (so far it would seem not).

High numbers should, in theory, have the edge on the new round mile course (1m9y), thanks to those on the inside being in the best position for the long, sweeping top turn. However, this hasn't worked out so far, stall 1 performing surprisingly well in big fields (this can only have been a fluke).

BEST EXAMPLES	7f9y
Soft	5292

LEOPARDSTOWN (L-H)

The course is about 1m6f round, with an uphill finish, and has a straight 6f track. High numbers are best in sprints, but low draws are favoured over 7f and a mile.

LIMERICK (R-H)

An undulating track of about 1m3f round, the course only opened late last year, so it's hard to be sure about any biases.

LINGFIELD TURF (L-H)

The draw advantage is nothing like as defined as it was in years past, and now only the odd meeting will be affected. The one factor that can have a massive effect on biases, though, is heavy rain falling onto firm ground, or simply firm ground (the stands' rail was clearly favoured at the one meeting to be staged on firm last year):

2109- **LINGFIELD** (L-H) (Firm (Good To Firm In Places))
Sunday June 24th
WEATHER: warm & sunny WIND:almost nil

2400 BET DIRECT FROM LITTLEWOODS MAIDEN AUCTION STKS (DIV I) (2-Y-O) **(Class E)** (11 Rn)
1:55 (1:55) **7f** £3,202.50 (£915.00; £457.50) Stalls: High

form		age-wt	dist	SP	OR	RR	SF
	1 Feathers Flying (IRE) DJSCosgrove dwlt: sn in tch against nr side rail: prog 3f out: led wl over 1f out: shkn up and sn clr: comf ....CRutter 11	2-8-1	---	10/1		79+	100
	2 Celtic Ballet MAJarvis dwlt: rr tl prog 1/2-way: rdn and hung lft over 2f out: styd on over 1f out to take 2nd nr finish ....PDoe 7	2-8-2	5	5/13		69	94
646-	3 Penneless Dancer [16] (1981) MBlanshard taken down early: led after 1f and crossed to nr side rail: rdn over 2f out: edgd lft and hdd wl over 1f out: no ch w wnr after ....DSweeney 1	2-8-8	nk	4/12		74	93

2401 BET DIRECT FROM LITTLEWOODS MAIDEN AUCTION STKS (DIV II) (2-Y-O) **(Class E)** (11 Rn)
2:25 (2:26) **7f** £3,202.50 (£915.00; £457.50) Stalls: High

form		age-wt	dist	SP	OR	RR	SF
0-	1 Fantasy Crusader [21] (1829) MrsLydiaPearce racd against nr side rail: chsd ldrs: rdn and effrt over 2f out: led over 1f out: wandered and jnd fnl f: hld on wl ....MHenry 11	2-8-7	---	40/1		84	99
00-	2 Red Oscar [13] (2043) SKirk sn outapced and pushed along: gd prog fr 1/2-way: rdn to join wnr ins fnl f: jst hld ....DaneO'Neill 4	2-8-6	hd	12/1		83	98
	3 Seamstress (IRE) PWHarris mde most: gng best over 2f out: shkn up and hdd over 1f out: fnd little: wknd fnl f ....PatEddery 8	2-8-4	3	5/41		74	95

2403 CRANSTON COMMUNICATIONS H'CAP **(0-70)** (3-Y-O+) **(Class E)** (16 Rn)
3:25 (3:26) **5f** £3,835.00 (£1,180.00; £590.00; £295.00) Stalls: High

form		age-wt	dist	SP	OR	RR	SF
114-	1 **Indian Bazaar (IRE)**[8] (2186) JMBradley racd centre: led after 1f: mde most after: jnd over 1f out: drifted lft fnl f: jst hld on ....PFitzsimons [3] 9	5-8-3	---	11/2[3]	48	**50**	107
301-	2 **Mousehole** [13] (2032) RGuest racd nr side: rr and sn pushed alng: no prog tl r.o wl fnl f: jst failed ....SSanders 14	9-10-0	nk	5/12	70	**71**	106
302-	3 **Absolute Fantasy** [10] (2120) EAWheeler trckd ldrs gng easily: rdn to join wnr over 1f out: hung lft and nt qckn last 100y ....SCarson [3] 6	b5-9-6	nk	14/1	65	**65**	106

Presumably because of the undulating nature of the track and the fact that the far rail is towards the bottom of a slope where it joins the round course, rainfall seems to make the middle and far side ride a lot slower. In these conditions, runners drawn right up against the stands' rail, often in only the top three or four stalls, have a massive edge.

On more than one occasion last backend, one side of the course seemed to be massively favoured, but this was entirely down to late-season ground. It was strange to see the far rail ride way slower on heavy ground on 5 October, though.

Concentrate On: The top six stalls on firm ground, the top three stalls if firm ground has been recently rained on.

LINGFIELD ALL-WEATHER (L-H)

The new Polytrack surface was opened in November last year, and it soon became obvious that the old Equitrack biases had gone.

From what's been seen to date, it seems horses can win from just about any draw over most trips. That may have a lot do with the lack of kickback making tucking in more comfortable for horse and rider.

A low draw is still advantageous over 6f with a front-runner, despite the course generally favouring late finishers, and jockeys willing to take the race by the scruff of the neck on such a horse can reap dividends. The distinct bias that used to exist over 1m2f does not seem there any more, with many winners coming from double-figure draws, something that would have been unheard of on the Equitrack.

To demonstrate how different the new surface is to the old, on 23 January Palawan became the first horse to win from stall 10 (the widest possible stall) over 5f since December 1996.

BEST EXAMPLES	5f-6f
Standard	5871

Quick Draw: The introduction of Polytrack seems to have put an end to biases.

LISTOWEL (L-H)

The course is flat and just over a mile in circumference. High numbers seem slightly favoured over 7f.

MUSSELBURGH (R-H)

It always used to be thought that, over 5f, high numbers were best when the ground was riding genuinely fast, and that the stands' rail (low) offered the best strip on good or slower.

That has probably still been true the last few years, but the recent trend has mostly been towards all runners coming centre to stands' side, whatever the going and whatever the field size.

That's unlikely to be what's seen this season, however, after Pop The Cork emphasised that the old bias still remained last August when winning easily from stall 17 of 17 on fast going. The only one to race up the far side, he was always well on top of a big group under the stands' rail, eventually winning by 2.5l.

The best strip of ground is definitely to be found under the stands' rail on good to soft or softer going, and the configuration of the course makes it very difficult for runners drawn above 8 under these conditions.

A high draw is preferable over 7f30y and a mile, particularly on firm ground, but it's very possible to win from lower down.

BEST EXAMPLES	5f
Fast	1105
Soft	682

Quick Draw: High numbers are best over 7f and a mile. Over 5f, when the ground is good to firm or faster, high numbers enjoy a definite advantage in fields of 14+; when it's good there's not a great deal in it, but on good to soft or softer, low numbers are clearly favoured.

Concentrate On: The top four stalls when there are 14+ runners over 5f (fast ground), the bottom six stalls on good to soft or softer ground. The top six stalls over 7f and a mile on firm ground.

NAAS (L-H)

The course is about 1m4f round with an uphill finish. While it's hard to be certain about any bias, there was a definite trend towards high numbers last backend.

NAVAN (L-H)

The round course has a circumference of about 1m4f, with sprints run on a straight 6f chute. High numbers have a clear advantage here.

NEWBURY (L-H)

When the ground is genuinely soft, it is not uncommon to see runners race wide down the back straight and down the side of the course in events of between 1m3f56y and 2m. In such circumstances, a high draw can become an advantage.

Many consider a low draw best in big-field races over the round 7f64y and 1m7y courses, since there is a sharpish left-hand bend into the home straight not long after the starts. While this is pretty much the case when the ground is good or firmer, it is definitely not true when the going becomes soft.

After a few races, the ground on the rail becomes chewed up and horses that are drawn high are able to race on the better ground (often only four or five horse widths off the rail) and swing onto the better strip in the straight. So while they are travelling that bit further, the surface is that much better.

High numbers are best on the straight course (particularly in sprints and particularly on heavy going), as shown by the last five years' results of the Weatherbys Super Sprint:

1997 LORD KINTYRE (7-1), 23 of 23.
1998 FLANDERS (6-5), 18 of 19.
1999 DON PUCCINI (10-1), 22 of 25.
2000 SUPERSTAR LEO (9-2), 18 of 22.
2001 GOOD GIRL (5-1), 15 of 25.

It's rare to see fields split into two groups, but that's what occurred in the race won by Cold Climate on 30 May 2001, and that race would offer an accurate guide as to the difference between the two flanks, the stands' side emerging 4.5l up on the far rail·

1428- **NEWBURY** (L-H) (Good To Firm (Good In Places))
Wednesday May 30th

1716 KINGSTON SMITH STKS SHOWCASE H'CAP (0-80) (3-Y-O+) (**Class D**) (21 Rn)
7:25 (7:30) **6f 8yds** £7,702.50 (£2,370.00; £1,185.00; £592.50) Stalls: Low

form		age-wt dist	SP	OR	RR	SF
405/	1 **Cold Climate** 292 (3560) BobJones racd stands side: drvn to take overall ld ins fnl f:r.o wl FNorton 19	6-8-1 ---	12/1	53	58	105
000/	2 **Wax Lyrical** 301 (3333) PJMakin racd stands side: tk overall ld over 2f out: hdd ins last: styd on same pce					
	....SSanders 11	5-8-13 2½	33/1	65	63	101
040-	3 **Full Spate** 7 (1531) JMBradley racd far side: led that gp ins last and kpt on: nt pce of same pce					
	....KDarley 7	6-9-1 2	5/1¹	67	60	99
/00-	4 **Fly More** 11 (1444) JMBradley srn chsng ldrs: led far side 1f out: kpt on same pce ins last					
	....PFitzsimons (3) 3	4-8-10 shd	25/1	65	58	98
056-	5 **Rafters Music (IRE)**9 (1461) BWHills racd far side and a chsng ldrs: kpt on same pce ins last MHills 6	6-8-9 shd	9/1	61	54	98
060-	6 **Mr Stylish** 9 (1459) JSMoore s.i.s and racd stands side: hdwy over 1f out: styd on ins last RHughes 20	vt5-9-9 nk	25/1	75	67	98
442-	7 **Bintang Timor (USA)**18 (1306) WJMusson b: lw: racd far side: bhd: hdwy over 1f out: styd on wl cl home					
	....PMcCabe 2	7-9-2 ¾	10/1	68	58	97
0/4-	8 **Eastern Venture** 19 (1268) WRMuir racd stands side: bhd: hdwy over 1f out: kpt on fnl f: nt pce to trble					
	ldrs ....KFallon 15	4-8-8 nk	8/13	60	49	96
6/6-	9 **Bundy** 18 (1306) MDods racd stands side: drvn and ev ch 2f out: wknd fnl f ....ACIark 17	5-8-12 1	14/1	64	50	95
0/4-	10 **Goodenough Mover** 13 (1382) JSKing led far side tl hdd 1f out: sn wknd ....RHavlin 5	5-9-11 1¼	10/1	77	60	93
004-	11 **Captain Gibson** 16 (1323) DJSFfrenchDavis racd stands side: chsd ldrs over 4f ....JReid 15	b3-9-3 3	20/1	78	53	89
0/0-	12 **Law Commission** 9 (1461) SKirk racd far: bhd: kpt on fnl f: gng on cl home ....PDobbs (3) 13	11-8-10 ½	20/1	65	39	89
001-	13 **Doctor Dennis (IRE)**5 (1586) BJMeehan led stands side tl hdd over 2f out: wknd fnl f BDoyle 6× 18	b4-9-5 shd	14/1	71	44	89
000-	14 **The Gay Fox** 9 (1459) MQuinn chsd ldrs far side over 4f ....JFortune 4	bt7-9-3 ½	33/1	69	41	88
112-	15 **Puppet Play (IRE)**56 (658) EJAlston chsd ldrs far side 4f ....WSupple 9	6-9-0 ½	6/1²	66	37	87
/00-	16 **Delegate** 14 (1372) NACallaghan gd spd far side 4f ....LNewman 10	8-9-13 ¾	16/1	79	48	86
000/	17 **Lakeland Paddy** 238 (4809) MBlanshard racd far side: a outpcd ....DSweeney 11	4-9-3 5	33/1	69	25	80
/00-	18 **Bayonet** 9 (1461) JaneSouthcombe racd far side: early spd ....ADaly 8	5-8-1 hd	40/1	53	8	79
1/0-	19 **Parkside Pursuit** 67 (526) MRChannon racd far side: sn outpcd ....CraigWilliams 14	3-9-2 nk	33/1	77	31	79
403-	20 **Supreme Angel** 9 (1461) KAWheeler racd far side: outpcd fr 1/2-way ....SCarson (3) 1	b6-8-12 1¾	16/1	67	17	77
0/0-	21 **Hill Magic** 13 (1382) LGCottrell racd far side: in tch to 1/2-way ....PatEddery 12	6-9-7 3	16/1	73	15	73

1m 14.61s (0.12) GOING plus 0.150 per fur (G) OWNER Mrs S A Jones (WICKHAMBROOK, SUFFOLK) BRED Juddmonte Farms
WEIGHT FOR AGE 3 from 4vo+ 9lb

Quick Draw: Runners drawn low in big fields generally struggle, whatever the going. Give preference to high numbers on the round course on soft or heavy ground, particularly after a few races have been staged.

Concentrate On: The top half in handicaps when there are 20+ runners, the top six stalls when the going is soft or heavy; the top six stalls on the round course on soft or heavy ground.

NEWCASTLE (L-H)

Early last season it was an obvious advantage to race as near to the stands' rail as possible in smaller-field races where they all came towards that side (front-runners enjoying a deal of success).

However, it was business as usual in fields of 14+ when they split into two groups, the far side coming out on top on all bar one occasion:

Firm – PRINCES STREET (1 of 20) beat runners drawn 2, 8 and 3. Nothing stayed stands' side.

Firm – TANCRED TIMES (3 of 18) beat runners drawn 5, 19 and 16. The stands' side were beaten 11+.

Firm – UNDETERRED (9 of 20) beat runners drawn 4, 3 and 1. The stands' side were beaten 6l+.

Firm – BLESSINGINDISGUISE (16 of 17) beat runners drawn 15, 12 and 1. Nothing stayed stands' side.

G-f – INDIAN SPARK (4 of 19) beat runners drawn 8, 3 and 7. The stands' side were beaten 6l+.

G-f – PRIX STAR (15 of 15) beat runners drawn 3, 1 and 4. This was the one occasion last season on which the stands' rail emerged successful (by 0.75l), and it came in late July, the month in which Newcastle and other courses (including Hamilton and Windsor) seemed to go rather wild with watering.

Good – TRINITY (19 of 18) beat runners drawn 18, 20 and 13. The field converged centre to far side, with those racing centrally holding a clear advantage.

Good – BABY BARRY (15 of 20) beat runners drawn 7, 5 and 14. Four stayed stands' side and were beaten 6.25l+.

Good – PATSY CULSYTH (9 of 17) beat runners drawn 8, 3 and 7. The stands' side were beaten 5l+.

G-s – SHARP HAT (9 of 19) beat runners drawn 7, 2 and 3. The stands' side were beaten 4.5l+.

Soft – SOME WILL (9 of 20) beat runners drawn 8, 2 and 1. The stands' side were beaten 8l+.

Heavy – DOWNLAND (4 of 18) beat runners drawn 15, 14 and 5. Nothing stayed stands' side.

Heavy – TARAS EMPEROR (11 of 18) beat runners drawn 3, 8 and 4. Four stayed stands' side and were beaten 4l+.

2533- **NEWCASTLE** (L-H) (Good To Firm (Firm In Places))
Friday June 29th
WEATHER: sunny WIND:fresh against

2567 NORTHERN ROCK GOSFORTH PARK CUP SHOWCASE H'CAP (0-105) (3-Y-O+) (Class B) (19 Rn)
7:00 (7:01) **5f** £19,500.00 (£6,000.00; £3,000.00; £1,500.00) Stalls: High

form		age-wt	dist	SP	OR	RR	SF
004-	1 **Indian Spark** 7 (2353) JSGoldie in tch far side: hdwy over 1f out: r.o wl to ld fnl 75y ....KFallon 4	7-9-10	---	7/2¹	99	107+	113
400-	2 **Get Stuck In** (IRE)²⁷ (1807) MissLAPerratt racd far side: mde most fl hdd fnl 75y: no ex RWinston 8	5-8-8	¾	25/1	83	89	111
/05-	3 **Ambitious** ²⁷ (1821) KTIvory racd far side: dwlt: towards rr: hdwy 1/2-way: r.o wl fnl f: nvr able to chal						
	....CCatlin (3) 3	6-8-10	1	14/1	88	90	110
344-	4 **Alegria** 8 (2396) JMPEustace racd far side: towards rr: styd on wl fnl 2f: nvr able to chal SHitchcott (7) 7	5-8-0	1¾	25/1	82	79	107
200-	5 **Ragamuffin** 9 (2315) TDEasterby racd far side: bhd: hdwy over 1f out: r.o wl ins fnl f: nrst fin TEDurcan 5	3-8-7	shd	25/1	88	84	107
/61-	6 **Atlantic Viking** (IRE)⁸ (2333) DNicholls racd far side: sn chsng ldrs: kpt on same pce fnl f						
	....ANicholls 6ˣ 11	6-8-11	¾	16/1	86	80	106
/00-	7 **Brave Burt** (IRE)¹⁴ (2177) DNicholls racd far side: w ldr: ev ch appr fnl f: wknd ins last .JCarroll 12	4-8-7	hd	33/1	82	75	105
000-	8 **Galloway Boy** (IRE)⁹ (2353) DNicholls racd far side: a chsng ldrs: no hdwy fnl f .AlexGreaves 10	t4-9-1	nk	25/1	90	82	105
/01-	9 **Connect** ²⁸ (1794) MHTompkins racd far side: sn towards rr: n.d ....KDalgleish (3) 6	4-7-13	½	12/1	77	68	104
362-	10 **Tadeo** ¹⁴ (2174) JMBradley prom stands side: led gp over 1f out: r.o: no ch w far side gp						
	....PFitzsimons (3) 19	8-8-7	shd	13/2²	85	76+	104
045-	11 **Night Flight** ¹⁴ (2177) RAFahey in tch stands side: chal gp ldr over 1f out: kpt on ins last GParkin 18	7-8-9	½	16/1	84	73	103
120-	12 **John O'Groats** (IRE)¹³ (2177) MDods racd far side: bhd fnl 2f ....JFanning 1	3-8-2	1¼	25/1	83	68	101
/05-	13 **Magic Rainbow** ³⁴ (1608) MLWBell racd far side tl wknd over 1f out ....MFenton 2	6-8-9	½	10/1³	84	67	100
105-	14 **Boanerges** (IRE)⁸ (2333) RGuest racd stands side: bhd most of way ....GDuffield 15	4-8-4	1	10/1³	79	59	99
315-	15 **Eastern Trumpeter** ¹² (2229) JMBradley chsd ldrs stands side tl wknd over 1f out .....KDarley 16	5-8-10	1¼	12/1	85	61	97
420-	16 **Henry Hall** (IRE)²⁰ (2400) NTinkler prom stands side tl wknd appr fnl f ....KimTinkler 20	5-9-5	nk	12/1	94	69	96
020-	17 **Elvington Boy** ¹⁴ (2174) MWEasterby led stands side tl hdd and wknd over 1f out .DaleGibson 17	v4-7-13	½	14/1	74	48	95
100-	18 **Sharp Hat** ⁸ (2333) DWChapman chsd ldrs stands side tl wknd over 1f out .....TWilliams 13	7-7-12	6	33/1	73	27	86
133-	19 **Absent Friends** ¹⁴ (2174) JBalding racd stands side: slowly away: a bhd ....JMackay (3) 14	4-7-10	3½	10/1³	74	17	80

59.20s (-2.44) GOING minus 0.150 per fur (F) OWNER Frank Brady (UPLAWMOOR, E RENFREWS) BRED H Young
WEIGHT FOR AGE 3 from 4yo+ 6lb

It's hard to know what effect the drainage work carried out recently – Vertidraining in both directions on the far side, and just one direction stands' side (against the way the horses run) – will have until we've had a few meetings. Perhaps it could swing things in favour of those to race down the centre, though – that was the case at the meeting staged on 24 August last year, when it was reported that 'work' had been carried out on the far side.

There have been 20 16+-runner 5f and 6f races staged in the past two years:

	top third	middle third	bottom third
Win %	30	30	40
Placed %	20	25	55

- Win percentages here are slightly distorted (14 of the 20 winners raced in the far-side group) and the placed stats better illustrate the bias.

Between 1996 and 1999, there were 28 qualifying races:

	top third	middle third	bottom third
Win %	14.3	25	60.7
Placed %	23.8	22.6	53.6

Six-year stats (1996-2001, 48 races):

	top third	middle third	bottom third
Win %	20.8	27.1	52.1
Placed %	22.2	23.6	54.2

- The bottom five stalls have been responsible for 46% of the winners, which compares favourably against the highest five stalls (just under 19%).
- If, in every race, you'd placed one point on the lowest stall, you would have made an 18-point profit.
- If, in every race, you'd placed a one-point reverse forecast on the two lowest stalls, you would have made a profit of just over 100 points.
- If, in every race, you'd permed the bottom three stalls in six one-point forecasts, you would have made a profit of over 400 points (139% profit on turnover).

BEST EXAMPLES	5f-6f
Fast	2606
Good	5090
Soft	1170

Quick Draw: High numbers are best in races when there are 13 or fewer runners (stalls invariably go stands' side) with front-runners having a good record. Low numbers did best in big-field (14+-runner) sprints whatever the going last season; expect the bias to reappear after a while even if it disappears early season following the drainage work.

Concentrate On: The top four stalls in sprints of 13 or fewer; the bottom six stalls in field of 14+.

NEWMARKET JULY COURSE (R-H)

The course is divided into two by a permanent rail, and racing is split pretty much between the two sides. Fortunately, it's now possible to know in advance of a meeting which side they'll be racing on, with the information carried in the *Racing Post* entries section (this only started last season).

Draw biases change here frequently, because there are so many variables affecting them (the best idea is always to watch the first couple of races at each meeting), not least the going, which has a total say on which side is favoured.

Here's a rough guide to where the best strip of ground can be found under varying conditions (remember that when 20 are declared, the stalls span the entire width, so their positioning doesn't make any difference):

**Racing stands'-side half, stalls stands' side (high)** – When the ground is riding genuinely fast, runners racing against the stands' rail (high) enjoy a huge advantage. On good ground, in big-field races, when the field splits, the stands'-rail is favoured over the far rail. When the going is soft, the stands' rail rides slower than the centre of the course, favouring runners drawn low to middle.

**Racing stands'-side half, stalls far side (low)** – Runners drawn high are usually favoured on any going, as racing out towards the centre is almost always beneficial to racing up the dividing rail. Occasionally, however, the rail will be favoured. Look out for the possibility of the top couple of stalls switching over to the stands' side in races with around 10 runners when the ground is riding fast.

**Racing far-side half, stalls anywhere** – The far side (low) is normally best whatever the ground, but particularly on soft ground towards the end of a meeting (that side is partially covered by trees).

BEST EXAMPLES	5f-6f	7f-1m
Fast	–	2368
Good	2971	–

**Quick Draw:** The odd meeting will crop up where one side of the course is favoured - i.e., the 2000 July meeting, where the stands' rail was much quicker - but biases come and go with regularity here. The best idea is always to look at what happened at the previous meeting. Also, always double check which side they're racing on and make sure the course don't decide to move the stalls mid-meeting, something they're inclined to do.

**Concentrate On:** The top four stalls when the ground is fast and they're racing on the stands'-side half and the stalls are stands' side (or there are 14+ runners); and the top stall in fields of around ten when the ground is fast and they're racing on the stands'-side half and the stalls are far side.

NEWMARKET ROWLEY MILE (R-H)

Only the odd meeting has shown a strong bias since racing resumed here (the course missed the entire 2000 season while the new grandstand was being built).

One such bias popped up at the Cambridgeshire meeting two years ago, when the far side had the advantage all week, but that can be put down to the fact that the grass appeared longer the further you came towards the stands' rail.

The permanent rail towards the stands' side usually comes down in time for the Champions Meeting but, while this used to have quite an effect (in favour of horses drawn low) lately the course seem to have cracked the problem and things have levelled out.

One bias here that some have trouble swallowing is that in favour of high numbers in big fields (25+ runners) over 1m4f, but results back it up, and the logic is there, as horses have less than a couple of furlongs to travel before meeting the long straight. High numbers also have a good record in the Cesarewitch.

When the going is soft, runners hard up against the far rail hold sway over those to race down the centre if the field stays that side, but those who tack over to the stands' rail are favoured over those staying far rail.

BEST EXAMPLES	2m2f
Soft	5387

Concentrate on: The top half in big fields (20+) over 1m4f and in the Cesarewitch. Watch for runners coming to the stands' side on soft ground.

NOTTINGHAM (L-H)

It was a huge advantage to race down the far side of the course in the spring of 2000 (at which time the stands' side looked to be riding 5-6l slower). Since then it's been a case of back in the old routine, in that only the odd meeting will show a bias.

It still appears that the stands' rail is best when the ground is genuinely firm, but that the centre of the course rides better than the far rail, which in turn rides better than the stands' rail when the ground is very bad:

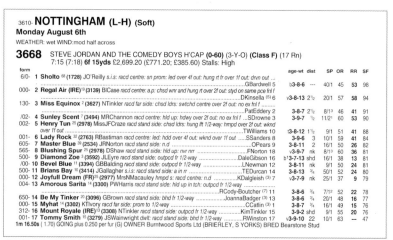

All that said, runners down the flanks (either top stall or the 1 box) seem to have quite a good record in sprints, so look out for jockeys who have shown themselves willing to go it alone in the past.

The theory that low numbers are best over 1m54y no longer stands up, and jockeyship seems more important round the home turn.

Concentrate on: The top six stalls in sprints on firm ground when the stalls are stands' side. Look for jockeys who have shown themselves prepared to go it alone being drawn in either the top or bottom stall in sprints (top and bottom of the shop have a good record).

PONTEFRACT (L-H)

Low numbers are best on good or faster going, since being drawn high in fields of 12 or more forces runners to either race wide and use early energy, or drop in behind and risk traffic problems.

The drainage work carried out in the home straight seems to have solved the problem of the ground on the inside riding slower on soft or heavy going. Last season it was something of a rarity to see anything switch to the stands' side off the final turn on bad ground (something that was invariably the case in the past). That said, those horses that chose to race wide from double-figure draws under these conditions did not seem hindered by it.

Keep an eye on the false rail – 4 metres outside the permanent fence – going up ahead of the fourth meeting of the season, and coming down again before the Friday fixture in mid-July. There have been 31 10+-runner 5f and 6f races staged on going worse than good in the past two years:

	top third	middle third	bottom third
Win %	48.4	35.5	16.1
Placed %	47.3	26.9	25.8

Between 1996 and 1999, there were 25 qualifying races:

	top third	middle third	bottom third
Win %	56	20	24
Placed %	50.7	25.3	24

Six-year stats (1996-2001, 56 races):

	top third	middle third	bottom third
Win %	51.8	28.6	19.6
Placed %	49.4	25.6	25

Over 37% of the above races were won by one of the top three stalls. This is roughly double what one would expect, with an average field size of just over 14 runners.

- If, in every race, you'd placed one point on the highest stall, you would have made a 41.5-point profit (74% profit on turnover).
- If, in every race, you'd permed the top three stalls in six one-point fore-

casts, you would have made a massive 374-point profit (111% profit on turnover).

Quick Draw: Low numbers are best on good or faster ground, particularly immediately after the temporary rail is removed before the Friday meeting in mid-July.

Concentrate On: Any horse that runs well from a double-figure draw on fast ground next time, as time often shows them to be ahead of the Handicapper, including Pertemps Fc, Baby Barry and Welsh Wind in 2001.

REDCAR (L-H)

A slight bias towards the far side (low) appeared last mid-summer, but it wasn't playable and didn't last long. It's not unusual to see fields verging on 30 several times throughout a season, but as often as not runners converge centre to stands' side, and previous straight-course form tends to be more important than starting position. Keep an eye on the weather forecasts before punting here, as westerly winds can have a serious effect on the watering (pop-ups).

RIPON (R-H)

The widely held opinion here has always been that on good to firm or faster ground you wanted to be up the stands' side in sprints, that on good ground there's never been much between the two flanks, and that on good to soft or softer you had to be up the far side. Ignore that, because results from the past two seasons (and particularly in 2001 – see below) and prove that you have to be high unless the ground is riding genuinely firm (when the stands' rail rides slightly faster, as shown by 2000 Great St Wilfrid).

3429- **RIPON** (R-H) (Good To Firm)
Saturday August 19th
WEATHER: fine WIND:mod half bhd

3796 WILLIAM HILL GREAT ST WILFRID STKS SHOWCASE H'CAP (0-105) (3-Y-O+) (Class B) (22 Rn)
3:25 (3:29) **6f** £24,375.00 (£7,500.00; £3,750.00; £1,875.00) Stalls: Low

form		age-wt dist	SP OR	RR SF
221/	1 **William's Well** 10 (3501) MWEasterby racd stands' side: w ldrs: led over 1f out: hld on wl towards fin ....DaleGibson 4	b6-7-13 ---	14/1 75	79 110
110/	2 **Blue Mountain** 14 (3395) RFJohnsonHoughton b: racd stands' side: sn drvn along: in tch: hdwy 1/2-way: kpt on wl fnl f: nt qckn towards fin ....KDarley 1	3-8-13 ½	5/11 92	95 109
221/	3 **Bahamian Pirate** (USA)8 (3560) DNicholls racd stands' side: a chsng ldrs: nt qckn fnl 150y FNorton 9	5-8-8 nk	10/1³ 84	86 108
602/	4 **Bon Ami (IRE)**14 (3395) ABerry b.hind: racd far side: sn outpcd: hdwy over 2f out: fnl rdn: edgd lft & kpt on same pce ins fnl f ....PBradley (5) 21	4-8-8 ¾	5/11 89	89 107
100/	5 **Cadeaux Cher** 14 (3395) BWHills b: racd stands' side: hdwy 1/2-way: styd on same pce appr fnl f ....NPollard 6	6-8-7 hd	12/1 83	83 107
135/	6 **Anthony Mon Amour (USA)**13 (3419) DNicholls lw: led far side over 1f: led far side over 1f out: kpt on same pce ....ClareRoche (7) 20	5-7-4 1	20/1 73	70 106
006/	7 **Boldly Goes** 12 (3432) CWFairhurst lw: racd far side: hdwy over 2f out: keeping on wl whn bmpd 50y out ....TWilliams 19	b4-8-5 shd	16/1 81	78 106
265/	8 **Amaranth (IRE)**12 (3432) JLEyre racd far side: sn chsng ldrs: nt qckn appr fnl f RCody-Boutcher (7) 22	4-8-0 nk	6/1² 83	79 105
315/	9 **Zuhair** 15 (3366) DNicholls b: racd far side: sn bhd: hdwy over 1f out: styng on wl whn nt clr run fnl 75y ....OPears 16	7-8-3 shd	16/1 79	75 105
200/	10 **Cryhavoc** 14 (3395) DNicholls b: racd stands' side: a chsng ldrs: one pce fnl 2f ......AlexGreaves 7	6-9-3 ¾	14/1 93	87 104
100/	11 **Pips Magic (IRE)**7 (3584) JSGoldie racd far side: hdwy whn nt clr run over 1f out: hmpd 1f out: styng on wl whn nt clr run & eased towards fin ....ACulhane 14	4-8-7 1	20/1 83	74 103
364/	12 **Further Outlook (IRE)**7 (3584) DNicholls led stands' side over 1f out: wknd ....GCarter 5	6-9-7 ½	10/1³ 97	87 102
101/	13 **Ambitious** 13 (3419) KTIvory b: racd far side: in tch: effrt over 2f out: sn wl outpcd ......CCatlin (7) 13	5-8-7 3½	16/1 90	71 98
436/	14 **Xanadu** 7 (3584) MissLAPerratt s.s: racd far side: racd keeping: hdwy to ld far side over 4f bhd & wknd over 1f out ....JMackay 15	4-7-11 shd	20/1 78	58 97
100/	15 **Double Oscar (IRE)**15 (3366) DNicholls b: racd stands' side: sn outpcd & bhd .....THamilton (7) 2	7-7-3 1	33/1 72	50 96
113/	16 **Friar Tuck** 12 (3432) NLEyre racd far side: in tch: rdn & edgd lft 2f out: sn wknd KDalgleish (5) 15	5-8-0 shd	14/1 81	59 96
001/	17 **Guinea Hunter (IRE)**28 (3033) TDEasterby lw: stumbled s: racd far side: a bhd ....JCarroll 18	4-9-10 1	14/1 100	75 95
404/	18 **Atlantic Viking (IRE)**12 (3432) DNicholls racd stands' side: chsd ldrs: edgd rt & wknd over 1f out: eased ....GDuffield 10	b5-8-6 ½	16/1 82	56 94
021/	19 **Sutton Common (IRE)**73 (1779) KARyan racd stands' side: outpcd 1/2-way: sn bhd IonaWands 3	3-7-10 ¾	33/1 75	47 93
040/	20 **Alastair Smellie** 14 (3395) DNicholls s.s: racd stands' side: a bhd ....JBramhill 8	4-8-0 1¼	14/1 76	44 91
000/	21 **Tara's Girl (IRE)**7 (3584) JJQuinn racd stands' side: sn outpcd: edgd rt & wknd 1/2-way PFessey 11	3-7-10 nk	40/1 75	43 91
300/	22 **Tadeo** 7 (3584) MJohnston racd far side: chsd ldrs: rdn & lost pl 2f out ....JWeaver 17	7-9-3 nk	16/1 93	60 90

1m 11.30s (0.40) (G) OWNER K Hodgson & Mrs J Hodgson (SHERIFF HUTTON, N YORKS) BRED M W Easterby And K Hodgson
WEIGHT FOR AGE 3 from 4vo+ 3lb

G-f — CLANBROAD (19 of 23) beat runners drawn 1 and 14. 14 stayed stands' side and were beaten 1.25l.

G-f — ATLANTIC VIKING (18 of 19) beat runners drawn 19 and 13. 13 stayed stands' side and were beaten 1.5l.

G-f — JESSICA'S DREAM (6 of 15) beat runners drawn 5 and 14. Ten stayed stands' side and finished 1.75l ahead.

G-f — DANAKIM (16 of 21) beat runners drawn 14 and 13. 12 stayed stands' side and were beaten 2l.

G-f — PERSIAN PEARL (1 of 16) beat runners drawn 15 and 14. Ten stayed stands' side and, although the winner came from that flank, she was dif ferent class, and the next one home was 6l behind the far-side group.

G-f — CAPTAIN RIO (10 of 14) beat runners drawn 12 and 11. Eight stayed stands' side and were beaten 15l.

Good — YOUNG BIGWIG (19 of 19) beat runners drawn 16 and 10. 12 stayed stands' side and were beaten 1.25l.

Good — CHARANGO (12 of 13, came stands' side) beat runners drawn 11 and 5. Only two went to the far side, from stalls 13 and 14 (an exposed 14-1 shot and a 100-1 outsider) and they were beaten 5.5l.

Good — ANTONIO CANOVA (17 of 23) beat runners drawn 23 and 1. 13 stayed stands' side and were beaten 1l.

Good — CONSENSUS (16 of 22) beat runners drawn 20 and 22. 12 stayed stands' side and were beaten 3.5l.

Good — AAHGOWANGOWAN (10 of 14) beat runners drawn 8 and 14. Nine raced stands' side and were beaten 1.5l.

Good — FANTASY BELIEVER (10 of 13) beat runners drawn 13 and 2. Seven raced stands' side and were beaten 3.75l.

Good — RESPLENDENT CEE (8 of 11) beat runners drawn 11 and 1. Six raced stands' side and were beaten 2l.

Soft — SERGEANT SLIPPER (11 of 16) beat runners drawn 16 and 15. Ten stayed stands' side and were beaten 3l.

Soft — FRANCPORT (1 of 22) beat runners drawn 12 and 14. The field were always spread across the course with no distinct groups formed, and the first one home from a high draw was beaten 2l.

Soft — NEEDWOOD BLADE (23 of 23) beat runners drawn 20 and 1. Nine stayed stands' side and were beaten 10.75l.

In the 16 sprints staged during 2001 in which fields split, the far side emerged successful on 13 separate occasions, despite the bigger group being under the stands' rail every time bar three.

The only three occasions on which the stands' rail came out on top were when Francport faced his ideal conditions in a strange apprentices' race, when Persian Pearl outclassed an average bunch, and when the first two home were Jessica's Dream and Fantasy Believer (from marks 32lb and 21lb below the ratings off which they ended the year respectively).

It's not essential to be drawn in the top two or three stalls, either. The best strip of ground seems to be between 4-6 horse widths off the far rail, with the above far-side winners coming the following positions away from top box: 5, 2, 6, 5, 1, 2, 7, 7, 5, 4, 4, 6 and 1. The cut-off point at which a 'field split' becomes questionable seems to be around the 13-runner mark.

In five 12-13-runner sprints staged last season, on three occasions the entire field elected to stay up the stands' rail (and another time only two went across). Predictably, the majority of these were juvenile events, when the inclination among jockeys is always to race with the main bunch.

Keep an eye out this season for which jockey is drawn in the top stalls in sprints of 10-13 runners. With a capacity of 23, a horse drawn in 12 of 12 (the stalls invariably go up the stands' side) is nearer to the far rail than the stands' rail to start with. Also, don't be surprised to see this become another Folkestone when the ground is riding good or softer, with all the jockeys electing to switch across.

High numbers are also best in big fields (18+ runners) on the round course, particularly over a mile. The best ground definitely seems to be on the inside round the top turn whatever the going, but particularly so on soft or heavy. Watering (by pop-up sprinklers) can be affected by the wind here, and while the management tries to avoid problems by turning them on at night, it's not always calm!

There have been 14 19+-runner 5f and 6f races staged in the past two years:

	top third	middle third	bottom third
Win %	64.3	14.3	21.4
Placed %	42.9	33.3	25

Between 1996 and 1999, there were 20 qualifying races:

	top third	middle third	bottom third
Win %	55	30	15
Placed %	50	25	25

Six-year stats (1996-2001, 34 races):

	top third	middle third	bottom third
Win %	58.8	23.5	17.6
Placed %	47.1	28.4	24.5

- 29% of the above races were won by one of the top two stalls. With an average field size of 21, assuming there was no bias, statistically one would expect a figure of just 9.5%.

- If, in every race, you'd placed one point on the highest stall, you would have made a 28-point profit (82% profit on turnover). Backing the second- and third-highest stalls would also have seen a profit.

- If, in every race, you'd placed a one-point reverse forecast on the horses drawn in the top two stalls, you would have made a massive 544-point profit (800% profit on turnover).

BEST EXAMPLES	5f-6f	Round
Fast	2333	2872
Good	4062	–
Soft	619 (2000)	–

Quick Draw: High numbers are definitely best in 14+-runner sprints, apart from on genuinely firm going, when runners drawn very low are favoured. When there are 10 runners or fewer, low numbers, who race nearest the stands' rail, are best. High numbers enjoy an advantage in big fields (18+ runners) on the round course, particularly at a mile.

Concentrate On: The top seven stalls in sprints when there are 18+ runners; the top five stalls when there are 14-17 runners; the top stall when there are 12-13 runners; the bottom four stalls when there are 11 runners or fewer; and the top six stalls over a mile in races of 18+ runners.

Avoid: Runners drawn down the centre in sprints.

ROSCOMMON (R-H)

The course is oblong-shaped and about 1m2f round; the draw seems of little significance.

SALISBURY (R-H)

Runners racing as near to the far rail as possible enjoyed a huge advantage (of around 6-7l over those down the centre) on fast ground in the early half of last season (up until the temporary rail was erected in mid-summer 4m inside the permanent):

1378- **SALISBURY (R-H) (Good To Firm (Good Final 2F With Good To Firm Patches))**
Tuesday June 12th
WEATHER: fine WIND:almost nil

2059 NATHAN'S H'CAP **(0-65)** (3-Y-O) **(Class F)** (20 Rn)
3:30 (3:34) **6f 212yds** £3,444.00 (£984.00; £492.00) Stalls: High

form			age-wt	dist	SP	OR	RR	SF
002-	1	**Inchdura** 5 **(1950)** RCharlton *lw: chsd ldrs: led over 1f out: pushed out* ....SDrowne 15	t**3-9-6**	---	2/1[1]	64	**75**	104
043-	2	**Kings Signal (USA)** 7 **(1873)** MRChannon *in tch: hdwy to chse ldrs fr 2f out: kpt on fnl f and tk 2nd cl home but no ch w wnr* ....TQuinn 18	**3-9-6**	2½	7/1[3]	64	**70**	101
/05-	3	**Definite Guest (IRE)** 7 **(1873)** GGMargarson *hld up in tch: qckned to chal gng wl appr fnl f: rdn and one pce ins last: ct for 2nd cl home* ....JFortune 20	**3-9-4**	nk	16/1	62	**67**	100
0/1-	4	**Egypt** 4 **(1994)** SirMarkPrescott *lw: pressed ldrs tl led o'r 3f out: rdn 2f out: hdd o'r 1f out: wknd fnl f* ....GDuffield 6x 2	**3-9-0**	5	7/2[2]	58	**52+**	95
/00-	5	**Prince Albert** 45 **(1010)** JRJenkins *s.i.s and swtchd rt to far side: hdwy on rails fr 2f out: kpt on fnl f* ....SWhitworth 3	**3-8-11**	1¼	33/1	55	**46+**	93
001-	6	**Piquet** 7 **(1874)** RHannon *chsd ldrs: rdn over 2f out: wknd fnl f* ....RHughes 6x 14	**3-9-5**	nk	12/1	63	**53**	93
105-	7	**Lushs Lad** 26 **(1379)** GLMoore *in tch: hdwy over 1f out: kpt on same pce ins last* ....IMongan (3) 4	**3-8-13**	1¼	33/1	60	**47**	91
/00-	8	**Myhat** 7 **(1873)** KTIvory *bhd: mod prog fnl 2f* ....SaleemGolam (7) 19	**3-8-10**	¾	50/1	61	**46**	91
0/0-	9	**Coccolona (IRE)** 13 **(1731)** DHaydnJones *bhd tl kpt on fr over 1f out: n.d* ....AClark 6	**3-9-2**	3	33/1	60	**38**	87
023-	10	**April Lee** 5 **(1950)** KMcauliffe *chsd ldrs: rdn 3f out: wknd 2f out* ....OUrbina 12	v**3-9-6**	1¼	25/1	64	**40**	86
/02-	11	**Ryan's Gold (IRE)** 8 **(1865)** MrsAJPerrett *lw: mid-div whn hmpd over 3f out: n.d after* .PatEddery 9	b1**3-9-7**	nk	10/1	65	**40**	85
000-	12	**Miss Beetee (IRE)** 7 **(1874)** JJBridger *bhd: sme hdwy fnl f* ....DKinsella (7) 7	**3-8-3**	2½	50/1	54	**23**	82
001-	13	**Aintnecessarilyso** 11 **(1771)** DRCElsworth *chsng ldrs whn n.m.r over 3f out: sn rdn and n.d after* ....DHolland 11	**3-9-7**	1¼	20/1	65	**31**	81
/55-	14	**Lucky Chrystal (IRE)** 57 **(773)** EALDunlop *chsd ldrs: rdn and edgd lft fr 2f out: sn wknd* GCarter 13	**3-9-0**	1¼	9/1	58	**21**	80
003-	15	**Saorsie** 8 **(1865)** JCFox *hld up: n.d* ....MFenton 1	**3-8-11**	¾	20/1	55	**17**	79
0/6-	16	**Young Tern** 45 **(1010)** CGCox *bhd most of way* ....JReid 5	**3-9-1**	nk	33/1	59	**20**	78
/00-	17	**Ela-Darlin-Mou** 11 **(1797)** KTIvory *chsd ldrs over 4f* ....CCatlin (3) 17	b1**3-8-11**	¾	33/1	58	**17**	78
/00-	18	**Majestic Quest (IRE)** 17 **(1725)** JNeville *led tl hdd over 3f out: sn wknd* ....SCarson (3) 10	**3-8-13**	1¼	33/1	60	**16**	76
000-	19	**Aunt Ruby (USA)** 13 **(1737)** TPMcgovern *chsd ldrs to 1/2-way* ....LNewman 8	**3-8-10**	3	50/1	54	**3**	73
320/	20	**Teenawon (IRE)** 292 **(3919)** GGMargarson *sn outpcd* ....GBardwell 16	**3-8-9**	½	50/1	53	**1**	72

1m 27.17s (-2.01) GOING minus 0.175 per fur (F) OWNER S M de Zoete (BECKHAMPTON, WILTS) BRED Stanley Estate And Stud Co

On soft ground the bias tends to swing full circle, when it becomes a case of the nearer the stands' rail the better (apart from in late season, when as at many courses the runner who finds the freshest strip of ground, anywhere on the course, tends to be favoured):

1147- **SALISBURY** (R-H) (Good To Soft Becoming Soft After 2Nd Race)
Thursday May 17th

1380 GERRARD MAIDEN STKS (2-Y-O) **(Class D)** (17 Rn)
3:10 (3:11) **5f** £3,770.00 (£1,160.00; £580.00; £290.00) Stalls: High

form		age-wt	dist	SP	OR	RR	SF
	1 **Doc Holiday (IRE)** BJMeehan *racd nr side: mde virtually all: rdn cir ent fnl f: r.o wl* ....BDoyle 7	2-9-0	---	9/2²		89+	99
	2 **Acclamation** LGCottrell *dwlt: racd nr side and sn rcvred: rdn to chse wnr over 1f out: edgd rt and no imp*	2-9-0					
	....ACIark 6	2-9-0	5	8/1³		73	91
-	3 **Glenmorangie** RHannon *s.s: plld hrd and hld up last far side: swtchd lft and prog 2f out: hung lft but r.o fnl f: improve*	2-8-9	2½	14/1		65+	87
	4 **Lucky Jacasa** MrsPNDutfield *racd nr side: prom: chsd wnr 1/2-way to over 1f out: fdd* CCatlin ⁽³⁾ 3	2-8-6	hd	14/1		59	86
0-	5 **Tappit (IRE)**¹⁴ (1070) MRChannon *led far side gp: no ch w nr side over 1f out: one pce* ...RHavlin 9	2-9-0	1¾	25/1		59	83
5-	6 **Woody Bathwick (IRE)**⁹ (1027) DrJRJNaylor *sn chsd far side ldrs: effrt 2f out: one pce and no ch nr side*	2-9-0	1¼	10/1		55	81
00-	7 **Keep The Silver** ⁸ (1225) APJarvis *racd nr side: pressed wnr to 1/2-way: wknd wl over 1f out* NCallan 1	2-9-0	¾	10/1		52	80
3-	8 **Eagles High (IRE)**⁸ (1225) RHannon *chsd far side ldrs: struggling after 2f: one pce u.p over 1f out* .	2-9-0	½	7/4¹		51	79
	....DaneO'Neill 13						
	9 **Wicked Uncle** RMBeckett *dwlt: racd nr side: m green and nvr on terms* ....DRMcCabe 4	2-9-0	hd	33/1		50	79
	10 **Filum Terminale (IRE)** MRChannon *chsd far side ldrs: wknd over 1f out* ....SDrowne 10	2-9-0	1¾	12/1		45	76
0-	11 **Lord Fernando** ¹⁰ (1179) GBBalding *prom far side: no prog 2f out: fdd fnl f* ....SCarson ⁽³⁾ 17	2-8-11	nk	25/1		44	76
	12 **Ewar Victoria (FR)** KOCunningham-Brown *dwlt: racd nr side: a bhd* ....DHolland 5	2-8-9	1½	33/1		34	73
	13 **Zeitlos** GGMargarson *m green towards far side and a rr* ....GBardwell 8	2-9-0	nk	25/1		38	73
0-	14 **Mint Approval (USA)**⁵⁴ (883) BJMeehan *racd nr side: prom to 1/2-way: sn wknd* ...GHannon ⁽⁷⁾ 2	2-8-7	hd	33/1		37	73
3-	15 **Mosspat** ¹¹ (1132) WGMTurner *w far side ldr to 1/2-way: sn wknd* ....GDaly 11	2-9-0	nk	16/1		36	72
	16 **Jacksmiles** JJBridger *s.s: racd far side: a bhd* ....RBrisland 16	2-9-0	3	33/1		27	67
	17 **Halland Park Lass (IRE)** SKirk *sed v slowly: racd far side and m green: wknd and eased over 1f out*	2-8-6	4	14/1		9	61
	....PDobbs ⁽³⁾ 12						

1m 4.21s (2.62) GOING plus 0.500 per fur (Y) OWNER Racegoers Club Owners Group (UPPER LAMBOURN, BERKS) BRED J Hanly

The confusion tends to start when the going is good to soft. Under these conditions one flank will often be favoured, but not always the same side, as shown by these results on good to soft from 3 October last season:

SHANTY (6 of 17, 1m) raced stands' side, beat the far side by a short-head.

DAWN INVASION (4 of 17, 1m) raced stands' side, beat the far side by 3l.

PASSION FOR LIFE (10 of 19, 6f) raced far side, beat the stands' side by 1.5l.

The rule of thumb has always been that high numbers are best on fast ground, that there isn't much in it on good to soft, and that low numbers take over on soft or heavy. Ultimately, that's still about the best guide.

BEST EXAMPLES	5f-6f
Fast	2056

Quick Draw: High numbers are best on fast ground, there's not much in it on good to soft, while low numbers take over on soft or heavy.

Concentrate On: The top six stalls on fast ground, the bottom six stalls on soft ground.

SANDOWN (R-H)

On the sprint chute, when the going is on the soft side and the stalls are placed on the far side (high), high numbers have a clear advantage. When the stalls are placed on the stands' rail, low numbers enjoy a slight advantage when all the runners stay towards that side, but when a few break off and go to the far side, high numbers again comfortably hold the upper hand.

Basically, the far rail rides much faster than the stands' rail, which in turn rides faster than the centre of the course. And, the softer the going, the greater the biases become, as shown by the race below, staged on dead ground.

4428- **SANDOWN** (R-H) (Good (Good To Soft In Places))
Sunday September 2nd

4448 RICHARD FREEMAN & CO H'CAP (0-75) (3-Y-O+) (Class E) (19 Rn)
5:30 (5:39) 5f 6yds £4,719.00 (£1,452.00; £726.00; £363.00) Stalls: High

form		age-wt	dist	SP	OR	RR	SF
552-	1 Days Of Grace ¹⁴ (4091) LMontagueHall chsd ldr tl led 2f out: hld on all out ....DaneO'Neill 19	6-9-2	---	11/2¹	62	66	106
600-	2 Speed On ²⁷ (3682) HCandy a chsng ldrs: drvn to go 2nd ins fnl f: kpt on: no ex last strides	8-8-7	1¼	20/1	60	60	104
	............CCavanagh ⁽⁷⁾ 18						
004-	3 Master Luke ⁵² (2961) GLMoore b: b.hind: bhd: hdwy on outside over 1f out: hung bdly rt ins last: fin wl	b4-8-3	½	16/1	49	47+	103
	............IMongan 5						
120-	4 Adweb ²⁸ (3656) JCullinan bhd: hdwy over 1f out: hung rt and r.o wl fnl f ....PDobbs ⁽³⁾ 6	3-9-10	shd	8/13	74	72	103
260-	5 Skylark ¹⁶ (4036) JLSpearing slowly away: hdwy on rails over 1f out: hmpd ins last: nt clr run and swtchd lft	4-9-2	hd	10/1	62	59+	102
	cl home: nt rcvr ....CraigWilliams 20						
530-	6 Fiamma Royale (IRE)²⁰ (3880) MrsPNDutfield led 3f: drvn to stay pressing wnr: hung lft u.p wl ins fnl f	3-8-11	hd	16/1	61	58	102
	............CCatlin ⁽³⁾ 17						
246-	7 Aintnecessarilyso ⁸ (4247) DRCElsworth lw: hdwy 2f out: chsd ldrs 1f out: chal ins last: snatched up cl home ....JFortune 16	3-9-9	1¼	11/2¹	70	63+	100
0/0-	8 Kingscross ¹¹⁴ (1274) MBlanshard slowly away: swtchd to far rails: hdwy over 1f out: nt clr run ins last: nt rcvr ....SDrowne 1	3-9-4	hd	33/1	65	57+	100
051-	9 Delegate ⁸ (4253) NACallaghan lw: s.i.s: hdwy 2f out: kpt on fnl f: nt pce to trble ldrs ....KDarley 11	8-10-0	nk	6/12	74	65	99
010-	10 Storyteller (IRE)¹⁴ (4080) MDods bhd: hdwy 2f out: rdn and kpt on fr over 1f out: nt pce to rch ldrs ..	v7-9-4	1	14/1	64	52	98
	............MRoberts 10						
000-	11 Woodlands ¹⁵ (4052) SDow v.s.a: hdwy 2f out: styd on fnl f but nt a danger ....PDoe 9	4-8-4	1½	20/1	50	33	95
600-	12 Byo (IRE)²¹ (3857) GMMccourt chsd ldrs: rdn 1/2-way: eddd rt 1f out: wknd ins last ..SCarson ⁽³⁾ 14	3-9-10	shd	33/1	74	56	95
000-	13 Dorchester ¹⁴ (4091) WJMusson bhd: hdwy and n.m.r 2f out: n.d after ....KFallon 3	4-9-10	½	10/1	70	51	94
605-	14 Rare Old Times (IRE)⁵³ (2933) MrsPNDutfield chsd ldrs: wknd fnl f ....GHind 12	3-8-7	2	33/1	54	28	91
500-	15 Ellendune Girl ⁸ (3871) DJSFrenchDavis hdwy 1/2-way: wknd over 1f out ....GCarter 7	3-8-13	nk	33/1	60	33	90
001-	16 Canovas Heart ²⁷ (3682) BobJones chsd ldrs tl wknd wl over 1f out ....GemmaJones ⁽⁷⁾ 15	12-8-10	shd	14/1	63	36	90
600-	17 Nautical Warning ⁴ (4363) JamiePoulton b.hind: sn outpcd ....RBrisland 4	l6-8-4	nk	33/1	50	22	90
064-	18 Miss Inform ²³ (3821) KOCunningham-Brown hdwy 1f out: wknd ....RMullen 8	3-8-5	nk	33/1	52	23	89
002-	19 Rushby (IRE)¹⁰ (4179) MrsPNDutfield b.hind: early spd ....LNewman 13	3-9-4	10	25/1	65	4	73

1m 2.38s (0.22) GOING plus 0.200 per f (G) OWNER Omni Colour Presentations Ltd (HEADLEY, SURREY) BRED Peter McCalmont
WEIGHT FOR AGE 3 from 4yo+ 1lb

It's doubtful whether the ditch, which has just been dug alongside the stands' rail on the sprint chute, will have any major effect on the draw. High numbers enjoy a definite advantage over 7f16y in near-capacity fields (14-16) runners, except when the ground is good to soft or softer, in which case jockeys invariably head for the stands' rail in round-course races.

BEST EXAMPLES	5f6y
Fast	3394
Soft	4091

Quick Draw: On the 5f chute, high numbers are always best in fields of 12 or more runners, particularly so on soft ground. In smaller fields, low numbers are best when the runners all stay up the stands' rail. High numbers are best over 7f16yds when there are 12+ runners, apart from on dead ground.

Concentrate On: 5f: (stalls stands' side) the bottom four stalls when 11 or fewer runners (the bottom three on good to soft or softer), the top stall when 12-13 runners on soft ground, the top three stalls when 14+ runners; (stalls far side) the top five stalls, the top three on soft ground; 7f16yds: runners drawn in double figures when 14-16 runners on fast ground.

Watch for: Front-runners racing next to the inside rail being favoured at any given meeting, as occurred on 1 September last year.

SLIGO (R-H)

The course is an oval of about a mile round, with an uphill finish. High numbers seem best at 6f.

SOUTHWELL TURF (L-H)

Low numbers should be favoured, but this rarely works out, as they are inclined to go too fast.

SOUTHWELL ALL-WEATHER (L-H)

The evidence of races run last year would suggest that the bias for races of between 6f and a mile continues to follow the same pattern as before. That is, a single-figure draw is an advantage over 6f, especially for front-runners and horses able to hold an early position, with the advantage gradually moving outwards as the distance increases.

Over 7f, stalls 5 to 8 are the only draws with a percentage strike-rate in double-figures since the start of 2001, while over a mile stalls 6 to 9 all have a good record. The theory that high numbers are best at 5f no longer holds water, those racing close to the stands' rail (stalls 11-16) having had an awful time of it of late. Some jockeys have enjoyed success by guiding their mounts right over to the far rail and racing alone over this trip, especially when the track rides slow.

At all three All-Weather tracks, it is advisable to look at the early results at any meeting to see if there is a bias towards, or away from, the inside rail.

BEST EXAMPLES	5f
Slow	5930, 5933

THIRSK (L-H)

While there's no doubting that Thirsk is not the bias course it once was, all the 12+-runner sprint handicap results from last season pointed to the stands' rail still being very much favoured on good or faster ground. This despite the course changing to an improved watering system a couple of years ago from the old pop-ups:

Firm – UPPER CHAMBER (20 of 19) beat runners drawn 15 and 18. Nothing went far rail, but the one widest out, Efidium (stall 1, won next time at 20-1) was beaten 5.5l.

Firm – EURO VENTURE (16 of 19) beat runners drawn 2 (Roses Of Spring) and 15. The far-side group were beaten 1l.

Firm – GENIAL GENIE (7 of 23) beat runners drawn 15 and 18. The winner went far rail, but with hindsight couldn't lose off a mark of 51 (finished 2001 on 72).

Firm – LYDIA'S LOOK (11 of 13) beat runners drawn 6 and 1. Nothing went far rail.

Firm – CUMBRIAN HARMONY (24 of 22) beat runners drawn 7 and 4. The far side were beaten 3l.

G-f – TECHNICIAN (21 of 22) beat runners drawn 13 and 12. The far side were beaten 3.5l.

G-f – SHOESHINE BOY (7 of 12) beat runners drawn 4 and 5. There was a bundle for the stands' rail in a smaller-than-ideal field; plenty found traffic problems.

G-f – JUWWI (21 of 21) beat runners drawn 18 and 23. The far side were beaten 1.5l.

G-f – TICK TOCK (20 of 22) beat runners drawn 16 and 24. The far side were beaten 3l.

Good – I T CONSULTANT (4 of 17) beat runners drawn 12 and 6. The winner raced far side on ground slightly slower than the official good, and this being an apprentice handicap, definite groups were never really formed.

Good – MARY JANE (5 of 15, switched straight to the stands' rail) beat runners drawn 10 and 12. Nothing went far rail.

G-s – GDANSK (23 of 24) beat runners drawn 1 and 12. The far side were beaten 1.25l.

G-s – PHARAOH HATSHEPSUT (1 of 21) beat runners drawn 6 and 9. The stands' side were beaten 4.75l.

G-s – AL'S ME TRAINER (11 of 12) beat runners drawn 9 and 1. Nothing went far rail.

4228- **THIRSK (L-H)** (Good To Firm)
Saturday September 8th
WEATHER: unsettled WIND:fresh half bhd

4601 END OF SEASON MAIDEN H'CAP **(0-60)** (3-Y-O+) **(Class F)** (22 Rn)
5:35 (5:37) 5f £3,517.50 (£1,005.00; £502.50) Stalls: High

form		age-wt dist	SP	OR	RR	SF
004-	1 **Tick Tock** [16] (4189) MMullineaux *mde all stands' side: hld on towards fin* ....ANicholls 20	4-9-3 ---	5/1[2]	48	51	101
000-	2 **Mr Bountiful (IRE)** [10] (4372) MrsJRRamsden *trckd ldrs stands' side: ev ch fnl f: nt qckn nr fin* ....RWinston 16	3-9-3 nk	10/1	49	51	100
004-	3 **The Old Soldier** [14] (4255) ADickman *lw: racd stands' side: bhd tl hdwy over 1f out: styd on wl towards fin* ....ABeech [3] 24	3-8-13 ¾	7/13	48	48	99
/42-	4 **Pride Of Peru (IRE)** [201] (327) MBrittain *racd stands' side: a chsng ldrs: nt qckn fnl 2f* .DAllan [7] 23	4-8-5 1½	10/1	43	38	96
000-	5 **Polar Haze** [20] (4080) MissSEHall *racd far side: chsd ldrs: kpt on wl fnl f* ....DMcGaffin [5] 6	v¹4-9-1 ½	12/1	51	44	96
533-	6 **Ho Pang Yau** [8] (4400) MissLAPerratt *racd stands' side: sn outpcd: kpt on fnl 2f* ..PHanagan [3] 15	3-9-11 shd	8/1	60	53	95
252-	7 **Sandpoint** [12] (4322) JGGiven *racd stands' side: sn outpcd: hdwy over 1f out: nvr nr ldrs* LEnstone [7] 19	l5-8-9 nk	4/11	47	39	95
3/0-	8 **Hermit's Hideaway** [226] (201) TDBarron *racd far side: hdwy 1/2-way: sn hrd rdn and outpcd* ....DRMcCabe 3	4-9-4 nk	25/1	49	40	95
000-	9 **Caposo (IRE)** [12] (4302) PWHarris *racd stands' side: a chsng ldrs: nt qckn fnl 2f* .RMullen 18	3-8-13 hd	16/1	45	35	94
500-	10 **Eddie Royale (IRE)** [40] (3486) DNicholls *swtchd rt and racd stands' side: sn chsng ldrs: one pce fnl 2f* ....JBramhill 11	3-8-12 1	50/1	44	31	93
004-	11 **Trudie** [15] (4233) MrsAMNaughton *swtchd rt and racd stands' side: sn chsng ldrs: outpcd fnl 2f* ....THamilton [7] 12	3-8-4 ½	16/1	43	29	92
300-	12 **Fiddlesticks** [61] (2865) MrsJRRamsden *racd far side: chsd ldrs: wknd over 1f out* ....PFessey 1	3-9-7 1	16/1	53	35	90
/40-	13 **Gill's Diamond** [14] (4236) NTinkler *racd stands' side: chsd ldrs: fdd fnl 2f* ....KimTinkler 22	3-9-7 nk	16/1	53	34	90
/00-	14 **Brew** [98] (1805) ABerry *led far side: wknd fnl f* ....GParkin 9	5-8-11 ¾	50/1	42	21	89
060-	15 **Chairman Bobby** [4] (4475) JeddO'Keeffe *s.i.s: racd stands' side: kpt on fnl 2f* ....DarrenWilliams [5] 17	3-9-8 shd	14/1	59	38	88
500-	16 **Crimson Bound** [15] (4233) RHollinshead *racd far side: chsd ldrs: edgd lft and wknd over 1f out* RMullen 14	3-8-13 1½	25/1	52	26	86
/00-	17 **Aster Fields (IRE)** [15] (4233) DShaw *sn outpcd and towards rr* ....JFanning 14	3-9-0 2	25/1	46	13	83
0/0-	18 **Highland Flight** [102] (1675) BobJones *racd far side: w ldrs tl lost pl over 1f out* ....TWilliams 8	3-9-7 ½	10/1	53	19	82
000-	19 **Anthony Royle** [10] (4368) ABerry *racd far side: sn outpcd and bhd* ....GBardwell 4	3-8-9 1	50/1	41	4	80
000-	20 **Kentucky Bound (IRE)** [12] (4302) JWPayne *swtchd lft and racd far side: in tch: hrd rdn 1/2-way: sn wl outpcd: eased fnl f* ....JCarroll 10	b3-8-12 nk	25/1	44	6	80
605-	21 **True Blade** [10] (4364) PFICole *racd stands' side: in tch: outpcd 1/2-way: sn lost pl* ...CCogan 13	3-9-0 1½	12/1	51	8	77
000-	22 **Needwood Trooper** [5] (3065) JBalding *racd far side: in tch tl lost pl 1/2-way: sn bhd: virtually p.u: t.o* ....DNolan [7] 2	4-8-11 dist	33/1	49	---	---

59.00s (-1.10) GOING minus 0.175 per fur (F) OWNER Michael Mullineaux (ALPRAHAM, CHESHIRE) BRED J A Porteous And C B B Booth
WEIGHT FOR AGE 3 from 4yo+ 1lb

A fair rule of thumb now would be that the stands' rail is best by around 3l on firm ground, by around 2l on good to firm, by 1l on good going, that there's not much between the two sides on good to soft, and that the far rail is best by around 3l on genuinely soft / heavy ground. In races run on the round course, low numbers are favoured over 6f216y and 1m whatever the going.

There have been 50 10+-runner 5f and 6f races staged in the past two years:

	top third	middle third	bottom third
Win %	48	28	24
Placed %	41.3	34	24.7

Between 1996 and 1999, there were 85 qualifying races:

	top third	middle third	bottom third
Win %	51.7	30.3	18
Placed %	43.4	31.1	25.5

Six-year stats (1996-2001, 135 races):

	top third	middle third	bottom third
Win %	50.3	28.9	20.7
Placed %	43	31.6	25.4

* Concentrating solely on handicaps, horses drawn in the bottom three stalls have won just 4.5% of the time (4 wins in 87 races).
* It is generally considered that the bias to higher numbers is more pronounced on firmer ground, and over the past six seasons, the statistics back this up. Of the 43 handicaps run on good to firm or firmer, the top third of the draw has provided 30 of the winners, which represents a strike-rate of almost 70%.

BEST EXAMPLES	5f-6f
Fast	3643
Soft	1131

Quick Draw: High numbers are best in sprints on firm ground, there's not much in it on good to soft, but low draws take over on soft and heavy. Low numbers are just about best over 6f216yds and a mile.

Concentrate On: The top four stalls over 5f-6f on good to firm or faster ground, the bottom four stalls on soft ground (14+ runners).

THURLES (R-H)

The course is undulating, oval in shape and about 1m2f round (the course doesn't stage any sprints).

TIPPERARY (L-H)

The course is 1m2f round with a straight 5f chute; low numbers seem best on the round track.

TRALEE (L-H)

The course is about 1m1f round, with a steep, uphill climb 5f out levelling out at the finish. High numbers seem to have a slight advantage over a mile.

TRAMORE (R-H)

The course, which is about a mile round, doesn't stage sprints, but it appears handy to have a low draw in staying events.

WARWICK (L-H)

Low numbers are slightly favoured in sprints on good or faster ground, but high numbers take over on genuinely soft or heavy going (particularly late in the season) at all distances. Under these conditions, the outside rail offers easily the best surface, as the ground on the inner tends to get chewed up.

Concentrate On: The top six stalls on soft and heavy ground. Look out for the more astute jockeys improving their position when flip starts are used on bad ground (the outside rail is best right round the course, at all distances).

Avoid: Any runners drawn above seven in fast-ground sprints.

WINDSOR (Fig. 8)

It is not uncommon to see large fields here right through the season, particularly in sprints, and there's a definite bias on every going bar good to soft, which seems to be the break-even point.

On soft or heavy (especially early season) it's a clear advantage to be drawn low and get as near to the far rail as possible; this can change somewhat in the autumn when, as at many other courses, it's a case of trying to find the freshest strip of ground.

However, high numbers are best on good or faster ground (particularly so on good to firm) and watering only seems to increase the bias further.

For some reason, watering here seems to loosen the ground, which invariably leads to unpredictable results and big-priced horses winning. However, all through last year, whichever runner managed to get hardest against the stands'-rail fence after the hosepipes had been out was at a huge advantage (see the sprints from 11 June below); clearly being drawn high makes this easier:

2043	SAFFIE JOSEPH MAIDEN AUCTION STKS (2-Y-O) **(Class E)** (19 Rn)

6:35 (6:37) **6f** £3,262.00 (£932.00; £466.00) Stalls: High

form		age-wt	dist	SP	OR	RR	SF
043-	**1 Decima** [8] **(1831)** PDEvans *racd against nr side rail: mde all: shkn up whn chal over 1f out: styd on wl* ....JoannaBadger [(3)] 17	2-7-10	---	10/13		71	---
340-	**2 Major Laugh** [13] **(1672)** BWHills *prom: chsd wnr over 2f out: rdn over 1f out and clr of rest: no imp fnl f* ....FNorton 15	2-8-4	1¾	10/13		71	---
	3 Bishop's Wood (IRE) MGQuinlan *hld up bhd ldrs: staedy prog over 2f out: outpcd by ldng pair over 1f out: styd on: nrst fin* ....TEDurcan 10	2-8-9	5	25/1		63	---

2044 RUINART CHAMPAGNE CLASSIFIED STKS **(0-75)** (3-Y-O+) **(Class D)** (12 Rn)
7:05 (7:05) **5f 10yds** £3,883.75 (£1,195.00; £597.50; £298.75) Stalls: High

form		age-wt	dist	SP	OR	RR	SF
14/	1 **Canterloupe (IRE)**[236] **(5060)** PJMakin *racd against nr side rail: cl up: plld out to press ldr over 1f out: rdn to ld last 150y: r.o wl* ....SSanders 12	3-8-6	---	8/13	75	80	105
002-	2 **Diamond Geezer (IRE)**[8] **(1836)** RHannon *racd against nr side rail: led: shkn up over 1f out: hdd and one pce last 150y* ....RSmith (5) 11	5-8-11 1½		7/21	69	78	102
1-	3 **Torosay Spring** [16] **(1593)** JRFanshawe *trckd ldrs: effrt 2f out: cl up 1f out: rdn and one pce fnl f* MHills 7	3-8-9 1½		7/21	75	73	100

2048 MLL TELECOM FILLIES' H'CAP **(0-75)** (3-Y-O) **(Class E)** (13 Rn)
9:05 (9:06) **6f** £3,066.00 (£876.00; £438.00) Stalls: High

form		age-wt	dist	SP	OR	RR	SF
423-	1 **Silken Wings (IRE)**[26] **(1370)** IABalding *racd against nr side rail: mde all: drvn and hrd pressed fnl f: hld on wl* ....MartinDwyer 13	3-8-13	---	4/11	64	67	---
/31-	2 **Pride In Me** [30] **(1307)** EALDunlop *trckd ldrs on nr side: plld out to chal 1f out: edgd lft and ev ch last 100y: jst hld* ....SSanders 11	3-9-7 ½		4/11	72	74	---
/26-	3 **Velvet Island (IRE)**[20] **(1484)** WJHaggas *hld up bhd ldrs: n.m.r on inner 1/2-way: prog 2f out: drvn and hung lft over 1f out: styd on* ....BMarcus 8	3-9-5 1		5/12	70	69	---

Over 1m67y, runners drawn high enjoy a slight edge, since the start is set on a chute and the course follows a tight right-handed loop to the point where it joins the sprint track. But ultimately, as often as not it's the jockey who gets right under the stands' rail who will emerge successful.

BEST EXAMPLES	5f-6f
Fast	1821
Soft	3680

Quick Draw: High numbers are definitely best in sprints when the ground is good or faster, there's not much in it on good to soft, and low numbers have a clear edge when it's soft or heavy.

Concentrate On: The top four stalls in fast-ground sprints, the bottom six stalls in soft- and heavy-ground sprints.

Avoid: Any runner drawn in single figures if there are 18+ runners over 1m65y and the going is fast.

WOLVERHAMPTON ALL-WEATHER (L-H)

Weather and harrowing has a big effect on the draw at all three All-Weather tracks, and nowhere more so than here. At the majority of meetings, there is a big bias towards those that make their challenges down the centre of the track, when staying on the rail is suicide.

Unfortunately, where jockeys choose to race has less and less to do with where they are drawn as the distance of the race increases, although horses drawn wide in sprints tend to stay wide. If power harrowing has taken place after particularly wet or cold weather, then the bias can switch to the inside, and under these conditions horses who race on or close to the pace also tend to be favoured.

Under normal circumstances, a middle to high draw is an advantage over most distances at up to 1m4f, and being drawn away from the inside rail also means you can escape the worst of the kickback. Always try to watch the first couple of races at any meeting, because any bias will soon become apparent.

BEST EXAMPLES	5f
Slow	5936

YARMOUTH (L-H)

It used to be a case of high numbers being best on fast ground and low numbers on soft, but since the course changed their watering system from pop-ups to a Briggs boom, things have become rather erratic, with the stands' rail looking the worst place to be if anything.

Although one side will often be favoured, there was little consistency last season, as shown by the results from the following races in which fields split:

G-f – (1 of 20) raced far rail, beat the centre by 2.5l, who beat the stands' side by 1l (the first home on the stands' side was Serengeti Bride).

G-f – HILLTOP WARNING (10 of 11) raced stands' rail, beat the centre by a head, who beat the far side by 25l (although only one went over).

G-f – CONNECT (6 of 10) raced centre, beat the stands' side by 14l (although only two came across and one joined the centre group mid-race).

Good – KIND EMPEROR (19 of 20) raced stands' rail, beat the far side by a head.

Good – INDIAN BAZAAR (6 of 19) raced far rail, beat the stands' side by 2l (Misty Boy, who won the stands'-side group, won next time).

Good – IDLE POWER (11 of 12) raced centre, beat the far side by 0.5l (Flying Millie, who won the far-side group by 9l, went on to win a better race next time).

Good – TAHITIAN STORM (13 of 13) raced stands' rail, beat the centre by 2l+ (first one home down the middle was Rapscallion).

Good – PEARLY BROOKS (6 of 19) raced far rail, beat the stands' side by 3l+, who beat the centre by 2.5l (same meeting as the above race).

Soft – PREMIER BARON (2 of 13) raced far rail, beat the stands' side by 7l.

The best idea remains to watch the first straight-course race at any given meeting and take it from there.

Quick Draw: The course used to struggle with off-shore winds messing up their attempts at watering but, since they changed to a new system, the problem has disappeared.

YORK (L-H)

It used to be thought that the main requirement in sprints here was to be drawn with the pace and not in the top few or bottom few stalls, but results suggest there's a bit more to it than that.

In fact, biases can be split up by ground - on soft ground the best surface is up the stands' rail, but on faster ground, there's a strip of ground bang down the centre that rides comfortably best. Check out the following 5f-6f results from last year.

(6F) HORSE	DRAW OF FIRST THREE	+/-	MEDIAN TIME
TAYIF	20, 4 and 9 of 23	(+2.31)	(dead ground and no draw bias)
MARSHMAN	2, 7 and 16 of 19	(+2.04)	(dead ground and no draw bias)
ORIENTOR	23, 13 and 22 of 20	(+1.42)	(dead ground and no draw bias)
ABBAJABBA	6, 2 and 1 of 21	(+1.02)	
JUWWI	14, 3 and 2 of 21	(-0.47)	(winner switched towards centre)
YORKIES BOY	6, 14 and 12 of 20	(-1.24)	(second and third progressive)
HONESTY FAIR	7, 2 and 4 of 15	(-1.53)	
PRISM	5, 6 and 13 of 18	(-1.61)	(third horse progressive)
TECHNICIAN	10, 5 and 4 of 23	(-1.88)	

(5F) HORSE	DRAW OF FIRST THREE	+/- MEDIAN TIME
PRIME RECREATION	2, 7 and 1 of 21	(+1.36)
SMART PREDATOR	9, 12 and 8 of 23	(-0.03)
AMERICAN COUSIN	12, 4 and 16 of 16	(-0.19)
EASTERN TRUMP'R	3, 1 and 2 of 15	(-0.95)
JESSICA'S DREAM	15, 5 and 9 of 20	(-1.30)

Basically, every horse that won a big-field sprint last season from a double-figure stall was either very progressive, or did so by switching out towards the centre.

Looking at the 6f results (knocking out those run on dead / soft ground), the winners were all drawn between 8 and 16 stall-widths from the stands' rail. So, when there are 15 runners on good or faster going, look to those drawn 1-7, when there are 16 runners, look to those drawn 1-8, 17 runners, those drawn 1-9, 18 runners, 2-10, 19, 3-11, 20, 4-12, 21, 5-13, 22, 6-14 and 23, runners drawn 7-15.

When the going is riding genuinely soft or heavy, it usually pays to look only to those drawn high (see Further Outlook's race from the end of the 2000 season opposite):

4828· YORK (L-H) (Heavy)
Saturday October 7th
WEATHER: raining WIND:almost nil

4865 CORAL EUROBET SPRINT TROPHY (HANDICAP) **(0-100)** (3-Y-O+) **(Class C)** (22 Rn)
4:15 (4:18) **6f** £25,642.50 (£7,890.00; £3,945.00; £1,972.50) Stalls: Low

form		age-wt	dist	SP	OR	RR	SF
003/	**1 Further Outlook (USA)**[13] (4612) DNicholls *mde all stands' side: kpt on wl fnl 2f* .....RWinston 16	6-9-11	---	14/1	97	102	108
050/	**2 Card Games** [14] (4604) MWEasterby *racd stands' side: a cl up: not qckn appr fnl f* ....TLucas 22	3-8-9	2½	16/1	82	80	104
001/	**3 Fire Dome (IRE)**[10] (4691) AndrewReid *racd far side: hdwy 1/2-way: led far side 2f out: nt qckn ins fnl f*						
	....MHenry 5	8-9-3	½	15/2³	89	86	104
120/	**4 Abbajabba** [10] (4691) CWFairhurst *a.p: stands' side: hdwy u.p 2f out: nvr able to chal* ..JFanning 12	4-8-9	1¾	4/1¹	81	73	101
026/	**5 Lago Di Varano** [13] (4612) RMWhitaker *led far side tl wandered & hdd 2f out: kpt on* DeanMcKeown 7	b8-9-2	shd	11/1	88	80	101
005/	**6 Royal Result (USA)**[21] (4451) DNicholls *a chsng ldrs stands' side: nt qckn fnl 2f* ..AlexGreaves 21	7-9-2	1	12/1	88	78	100
040/	**7 Kayo** [21] (4451) MJohnston *racd far side: prom: chal 2f out: btn 1f out* ....DHolland 6	5-9-12	3	20/1	98	80	96
200/	**8 Ivory Dawn** [21] (4468) KTIvory *racd far side: hdwy 2f out: nvr able to chal* ....CCarver [3] 8	4-8-9	3½	20/1	78	50	91
050/	**9 Cauda Equina** [4] (4776) MRChannon *s.i.s: racd far side: outpcd tl sme late hdwy* ....RMullen 4	6-8-9	1½	25/1	81	49	89
000/	**10 Bon Ami (IRE)**[13] (4612) ABerry *racd far side: cl up tl wknd wl over 1f out* ....PBradley [5] 2	4-8-11	½	20/1	88	55	88
010/	**11 Zuhair** [21] (4451) DNicholls *racd far side: sn outpcd: sme late hdwy: n.d* ....FNorton 1	7-8-12	½	20/1	84	50	88
200/	**12 Marsad (IRE)**[21] (4451) JAkehurst *reard s: sn chsng ldrs far side: wknd fnl 2f* ....PDoe 9	6-9-2	hd	10/1	88	53	87
004/	**13 Juwwi** [10] (4691) JMBradley *racd stands' side: s.i.s: nvr rchd ldrs* ....MSavage [7] 13	6-8-7	2	7/1²	86	46	85
300/	**14 Friar Tuck** [21] (4449) MissLAPerratt *cl up far side 4f: wknd* ....KDalgleish [5] 3	5-8-3	hd	25/1	80	40	85
050/	**15 Debbie's Warning** [56] (3590) KMahdi *racd stands' side: outpcd after 2f* ....SWhitworth 19	4-9-1	1½	33/1	87	43	83
050/	**16 Karameg (IRE)**[22] (4430) PWHarris *swtchd &: racd stands' side: cl up tl wknd fr 1/2-way* .....ABeech [3] 10	4-8-7	6	20/1	82	22	75
400/	**17 Return Of Amin** [63] (3395) WRMuir *racd stands' side: sn outpcd* ....MartinDwyer 14	b6-8-7	½	16/1	79	17	74
230/	**18 Brecongill Lad** [31] (4258) DNicholls *racd far side: w ldrs 4f: wknd* ....ANicholls 18	8-9-1	5	16/1	87	12	67
000/	**19 First Maite** [8] (4732) SRBowring *racd centre: prom tl outpcd fnl 2f* ....GDuffield 11	vt7-9-0	hd	20/1	86	11	67
100/	**20 Loch Inch** [101] (2350) MTebbutt *dwlt: racd stands' side: n outpcd* ....MTebbutt 20	b3-9-0	½	50/1	87	10	66
000/	**21 Fearby Cross (IRE)**[21] (4449) WJMusson *racd stands' side: sn outpcd* ....LNewton 15	4-8-6	2½	12/1	78	---	63
000/	**22 Pips Magic (IRE)**[14] (4597) JSGoldie *racd stands' side: in tch 4f* ....ACulhane 23	4-8-9	1¾	33/1	81	---	61

1m 18.74s (8.24) GOING plus 1.225 per fur (S) OWNER Mark A Leatham (SESSAY, N YORKS) BRED Gainsborough Farm Inc
WEIGHT FOR AGE 3 from 4yo+ 1lb

The bias towards low numbers on the round course is well documented and tends to stand up well (although not so much in last year's John Smith's Cup for some reason) apart from on late-season, dead ground. One additional factor that can greatly accentuate the round-course bias is the over-watering of firm ground, when it's a case of the nearer the inside, the better.

BEST EXAMPLES	5f-6f	Round
Fast	4531	–
Good	2174	2854 (2000)

Quick Draw: Runners drawn in the top half tend to struggle in big-field sprints when the ground is good or faster, but runners drawn high (near the stands' rail) are favoured when it's soft or heavy. Low numbers are best on the round course at distances up to and including 1m2f85yds.

Concentrate On: Runners drawn around 12 stalls away from the stands' rail in sprints on good or faster ground; the top six stalls in soft / heavy-ground sprints; the bottom six stalls in big-field races of up to 1m2f85yds when the ground is good or faster.

2001 RACECOURSE CONCLUSIONS

Draw biases have changed dramatically at several courses in the past couple of years, often as a result of new watering systems.

The top-ten bias list in *Backing the Draw for Profit* (2000) was as follows:
1. Beverley
2. Hamilton (soft)
3. Ripon
4. Sandown (soft)
5. Folkestone
6. Kempton (soft)
7. Thirsk (firm)
8. Windsor
9. Newcastle
10. Catterick

Here are the revised lists:

GRAHAM WHELDON
1. Beverley (5f, good or faster ground, high)
2. Chepstow (5f-1m, high)
3. Ripon (5f-6f)
4. Windsor (5f-6f, fast (watered) ground, high)
5. Chester (low)
6. Folkestone (straight course, high)
7. Musselburgh (5f, fast ground, 14+ runners, high)
8. Curragh (5f-6f)
9. Thirsk (5f-6f, fast ground, high)
10. Newcastle (5f-6f)

DAVID RENHAM
1. Beverley (5f, good or faster ground, high)
2. Chester (low)
3. Chepstow (5f-1m, high)
4. Folkestone (straight course, soft, high)
5. Goodwood (7f, good or faster, high)
6. Ripon (5f-6f, 19+ runners, high)
7. Newcastle (5f-6f, 16+ runners, low)
8. Thirsk (5f-6f, fast ground, high)
9. Epsom (1m114y, low)
10. Ayr (1m, fast ground, low)

CHAPTER 2

Racecourses

Distances open to change when 'dolling out' occurs are shown in **bold**.
Dolling out (moving the inside rail) can cause the actual race distance to
vary from the distance shown. Such races are advertised in the racing
press prefixed by the word 'about'.

Excuse the drainage jargon, but I'm not sufficiently up to speed with
these things to be able to explain them in detail. Essentially, though,
Vertidraining is similar to sand-slitting, but the former goes to a depth of
approximately 14 inches, while the latter goes to only 6 inches.

ASCOT

Stalls: go on the stands' side (low) nine times out of ten on the straight course. If the ground gets very soft, problems can occur in the 7f and 1m (st) areas and flip starts become an option.

Rails: both rails on the straight course, which is about 35 metres wide at the mile start and gradually diminishes, used to be permanent, but each can now be moved by up to 5 metres. How much they are depends on the meeting.

Straight course points: west.

Watering: is done by an Upton irrigator (pop-up sprinklers are used in an emergency and on the round course).

Drainage: compaction is reduced by Vertidraining and slitting.

Maximum runners: 5f (28), 6f (30), 6f110y (30), 7f (30), 1m (st) (32), 1m (rnd) (30), **1m2f** (18), 1m4f (20), **2m45y** (20), **2m4f** (29), **2m6f34y** (32).

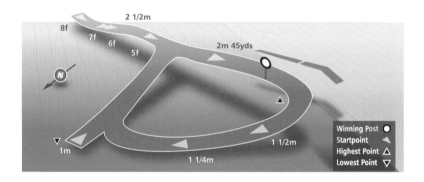

AYR

Stalls: normally go on the stands' rail (high) in races at up to 6f, although they are occasionally put on the far rail (low) to preserve the ground stands' side. For a trial period here (and at many other courses), they were placed down the centre, but apparently this proved unpopular with trainers.

Rails: the course is slightly narrower, at 29 metres, than before because of the introduction of aluminium rails. All rails can be moved, and are frequently (by up to 3 metres) dependent on ground conditions.

Sprint course points: north-west.

Watering: a Briggs boom is now used, and has proven successful as it is slow-moving, covers the full width of the track, and is not effected by the wind, which blows off the sea.

Drainage: no major work has been carried out recently.

Maximum runners: 5f (20, 27 at Western Meeting), 6f (20, 29 at Western Meeting), **7f50y** (18), **1m** (20), **1m1f20y** (20), **1m2f** (20), **1m2f192y** (20), **1m5f13y** (20), **1m7f** (20), **2m1f105y** (20).

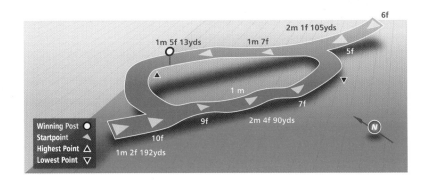

BATH

Stalls: go on the inside (low) over all distances.

Rails: realignment work was carried out on the home turn in 1994/1995 and, while both rails can now be moved, this is not the preferred method, and they tend to construct false rails by dolling out where necessary. The 5f11y start is about 34 metres wide, considerably wider than the 5f161y start, which is only 19 metres across.

Straight points: west.

Watering: because of its height above sea level, the course is unique in having no watering system.

Drainage: just basic spiking.

Maximum runners: 5f11y (20), **5f161y** (19), **1m5y** (16), **1m2f46y** (20), **1m3f144y** (20), **1m5f22y** (15), **2m1f34y** (20).

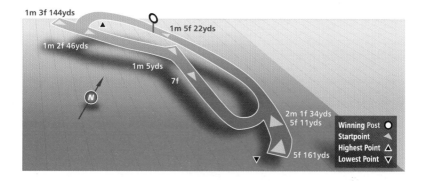

BEVERLEY

Stalls: go on the inside rail (high). Flip starts are not uncommon over 5f, since it is difficult for the stalls to be moved across the centre of the course to the starting point when the ground is wet.

Rails: the rails in the straight course, which is about 31 metres wide and faces west, are not moved. However, the rail on the far bend was moved about 3 yards last summer for about six meetings, in order to give some 'chewed-up ground' time to recover (it was back in its usual position come the autumn).

Sprint course points: west.

Watering: a dragline is used and can be adjusted to offset wind effects.

Drainage: some drainage work was carried out at the end of 2001 round the home bend, while in the 1999 close season gravel-banding was carried out in the final furlong (as it had been six years ago). The last furlong had ridden slow, but should now be faster.

Maximum runners: **5f** (20), **7f100y** (17), **1m100y** (19), **1m1f207y** (19), **1m3f216y** (15), **2m35y** (20).

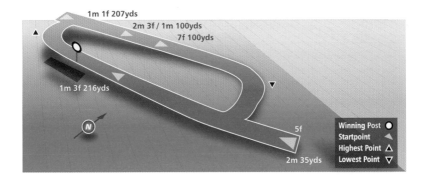

BRIGHTON

Stalls: go on the inside (low) except at the 1m1f209y and 1m3f196y starts, when they go on the outside (due to the configuration of the track the Jockey Club inspectors will not sanction any other positioning).

Rails: the width of the course at the 5f59y start is approximately 21 metres, and the rails are sometimes moved to lessen wear and tear (dolling off by up to 4 metres makes little difference to race distances, since the course turning left and right balances things out).

Straight points: south-west (the same direction as that in which the pre-vailing wind from off the sea comes).

Watering: a Briggs boom is used, and any wind effect is therefore slight.

Drainage: the course is based on chalk soil, so no drainage work has been required (apparently it drains at 12 inches an hour).

Maximum runners: 5f59y (16, 14 when dolled), **5f213y** (18, 16 when dolled), **6f209y** (18, 16 when dolled), **7f214y** (15), **1m1f209y** (20), **1m3f196y** (18).

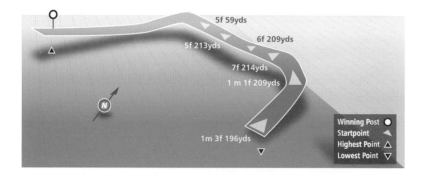

CARLISLE

Stalls: normally go on the inside (high) at all distances, although they sometimes go down the centre in sprints.

Rails: The rails are moveable, by up to about 3 metres (compared to only 1 metre ahead of last season) when the ground is really cut up, but this rarely happens. The sprint course is about 22 metres wide.

Sprint course points: east, and the prevailing wind is normally westerly.

Watering: a 'gun' system is in place, but has yet to be used, thanks to F&M.

Drainage: sand-slits were put in all over the place at the end of the 2000 season, and again through the last 2f last season. Vertidrain is done twice a year and a spiker is used.

Maximum runners: **5f** (20), **5f207y** (20), **6f206y** (15), **7f214y** (18), **1m1f61y** (16), **1m4f** (20), **1m6f32y** (14), **2m1f52y** (18).

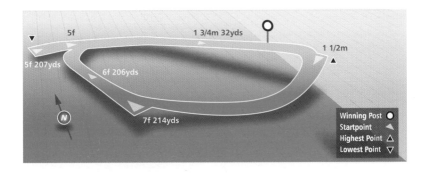

CATTERICK

Stalls: usually go on the far rail (low) at all distances, including at 5f212y, a trip at which they were invariably positioned on the outer (high) before last year.

Rails: the inside rail can be moved by as much as 3 metres in the home straight (which is between 24 and 28 metres wide) and on the home bend by as much as 4-5 metres. This is normally done in the autumn to preserve the ground for the following spring but no need last year thanks to F&M shortening the season. The stands' rail up the straight course is permanent.

Sprint course points: north-west.

Watering: towlines are used, and can be adjusted to offset the effects of the wind.

Drainage: the home bend has been gravel-banded in an attempt to improve drainage, while the patches that needed it were Vertidrained over the winter.

Maximum runners: 5f (17, temp 12), **5f212y** (14, temp 12), **7f** (18, temp 15), **1m3f214y** (20, temp 17), **1m5f175y** (17, temp 12), **1m7f177y** (20, temp 15).

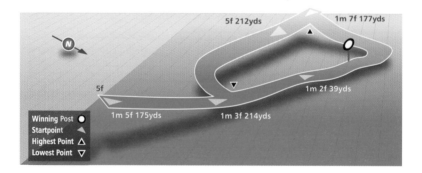

CHEPSTOW

Stalls: always go on the stands' side (high) at up to 1m14y.

Rails: the rails in the straight course, which is 24 metres wide, are permanent. There is no inside rail down the back straight until after the landing side of the final fence.

Straight course points: south-east.

Watering: towlines are used and can be adjusted to offset any wind effects. This was due to be updated in April (this year), hopefully with the effect of doubling the water capacity.

Drainage: the course in based on sandstone, so draining is excellent, and Vertidraining is only required occasionally. This year, the course will be using a new 'earthquake' machine for de-compacting the ground.

Maximum runners: 5f16y (20), 6f16y (20), 7f16y (20), 1m14y (20), **1m2f36y** (16), **1m4f23y** (19), **2m49y** (16), 2m2f (18).

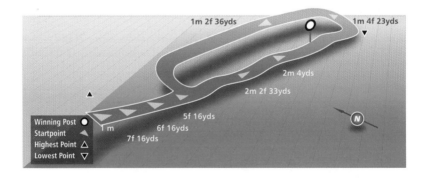

CHESTER

Stalls: go on the inside (low), except for races run over 1m2f75y and 2m2f117y (same starting points) where they are put on the outside. However, sometimes the stalls will be advertised as low in all races, but the starter (dependent upon who it is) may have them pushed nearer the centre, especially over 5f, in a bid to offset the strong low bias. The ground can become wet enough for flip starts to become necessary.

Rails: the inside rail can be moved, from the 51/2f from home point to the furlong pole, going out by as much as 4 metres at the furthest point, and usually is on the Thursday of the May meeting. Plans are afoot this year to doll out further when and where necessary.

Straight points: north-west.

Watering: a computer-operated pop-up system is used and the wind has little or no effect (they try to water well in advance of a meeting in any case).

Drainage: sand-slits have been installed between the 2f and 4f points, and further drainage work may take place just before racing resumes. Vertidraining is carried out once a year and spiking is done regularly during the season.

Maximum runners: 5f16y (16), 6f18y (16), 7f2y (16), 7f122y (18), 1m2f75y (17), 1m3f79y (16), 1m4f66y (16), 1m5f89y (16), 1m7f195y (18), 2m2f147y (18).

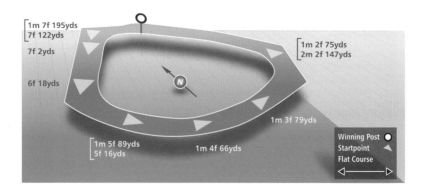

DONCASTER

Stalls: normally go on the stands' rail (high) in the straight, and on the inside rail (low) at distances of 1m2f60y and beyond. Over the round mile, they are now placed on the outside, since during a trial period in 1996 when they were placed on the inside it was found that jockeys on runners drawn high were inclined to chop off those on the inner.

Rails: the straight course is about 25 metres wide at the mile start, tapering down to 18 metres at the winning post. The rails are never moved on the straight course, but a 'false' can be used on the round course (outside the permanent by up to 5 metres).

Straight course points: west.

Watering: towlines are used and watering is done 1 metre off the rail to offset the wind effect.

Drainage: no recent major drainage work has been carried out, just Vertidraining when necessary, and slitting / spiking during the summer prior to watering.

Maximum runners: 5f (22), 5f 140y (22), 6f (22), **6f110y** (22), 7f (22), 1m (st) (24), **1m (rnd)** (25, 20 when dolled), **1m2f60y** (20), **1m4f** (24, 19 when dolled), **1m6f132y** (24, 20 when dolled), **2m110y** (18), **2m2f** (20).

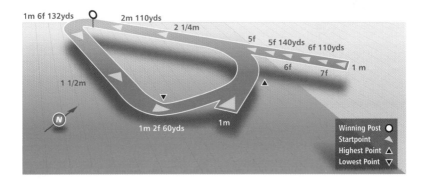

EPSOM

Stalls: invariably go up the stands' side (high) over 5f and over 6f (which starts on a chute), in the centre at the Derby start and on the inside (low) for races at between 7f and 1m2f.

Rails: the rails are moveable for the few races staged on the 5f course, which is 35 metres wide, and whether they are depends upon how much racing has been staged on the round course.

Sprint course points: west.

Watering: the course now uses a Briggs boom for the back and home straight, and towlines round Tattenham corner (prior to 2001 it had been all towlines).

Drainage: no major work has been needed in recent seasons.

Maximum runners: 5f (20), **6f** (17), **7f** (17), **1m114y** (20), **1m2f18y** (30), **1m4f10y** (30).

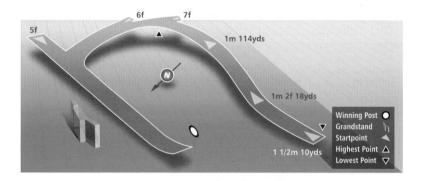

FOLKESTONE

Stalls: usually go on the stands' rail (low) for straight races.

Rails: the rails in the straight course, which is 23 metres wide, are never moved (they are occasionally on the round course).

Straight course points: east.

Watering: is achieved by towlines.

Drainage: no major work has been necessary over the past two seasons (none is planned, either, in the near future). Vertidraining is carried out annually.

Maximum runners: 5f (16), 6f (16), **6f189y** (16), **7f** (16), **1m1f149y** (15), **1m4f** (18), **1m7f 92y** (16), **2m93y** (16).

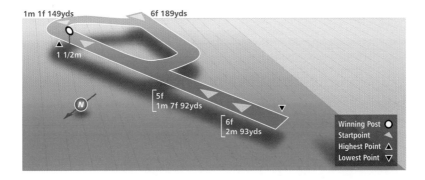

GOODWOOD

Stalls: go on the stands' side (low) wherever possible on the straight course (which is 31 metres wide) and are only switched to the far rail in exceptional circumstances (ie, very heavy ground, which hasn't been seen in years).

Rails: the stands' rail is permanent, but a 'temporary' is frequently employed up the far side to bring the course in by up to 5 metres, right down to the winning post.

Sprint course points: south.

Watering: an Upton irrigator is used, so the wind has no major effect.

Drainage: intensive turf management has been carried out on the top bend re-entering the straight, and the course also Vertidrain every autumn and at the end of June in time for the Glorious meeting.

Maximum runners: 5f (28), 6f (30), **7f** (20), **1m** (22), **1m1f** (20), **1m1f192y** (20), **1m3f** (16), **1m4f** (16), **1m6f** (17), **2m** (16), **2m4f** (20), **2m5f** (20).

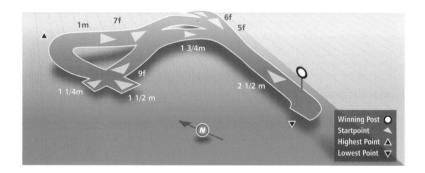

HAMILTON

Stalls: go on the stands' side (low) on the straight course.

Rails: the inside rail on the 'loop' can be moved by up to 10 metres, but both rails in the straight, which is about 22 metres wide, are permanent.

Sprint course points: north-west.

Watering: an Upton irrigator is used.

Drainage: quite a bit of work has been done recently, including sand-slitting from half a furlong out to halfway round the pull-up, and in the dip at the top of the 'loop' (about 3f110y out). Vertidraining is done every season.

Maximum runners: 5f4y (18), 6f5y (18), **1m65y** (16), **1m1f36y** (18), **1m3f16y** (18), **1m4f17y** (18), **1m5f9y** (18).

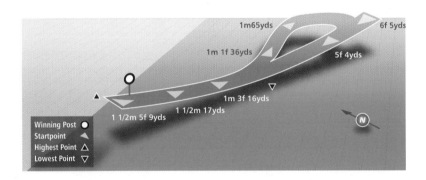

HAYDOCK

Stalls: now tend to go down the centre, rather than their traditional stands' side (high) position on the straight course.

Rails: The rails in the straight, which is about 26 metres wide, are rarely moved, and only usually are to avoid very wet patches, particularly at the 4f marker (flip starts are occasionally seen, most frequently at the 7f and mile starts).

Sprint course points: west.

Watering: is done by an Upton irrigator, so the wind effect is minimal.

Drainage: an enormous amount of work was done in the winter of 2000 between the 5f and 6f points, with 6mm gravel drains put in. Vertidraining is now only carried out once a year, and a new connector drain been inserted, which drains water off to the local river.

Maximum runners: 5f (24), 6f (24), **7f30y** (16), **1m30y** (18), **1m2f120y** (20), **1m3f200y** (20), **1m6f** (20), **2m45y** (20).

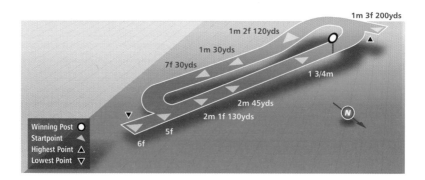

KEMPTON

Stalls: position is alternated between the far rail (high) and the stands' rail (low) on the sprint course. As a rule of thumb, when the ground is slower than good, they tend to go on the far side, and when it's good or quicker they go stands' side.

Rails: neither rail on the separate sprint chute, which is about 30 metres wide, is moveable.

Sprint chute points: south-west.

Watering: pop-up sprinklers are used, but there is a slight overlap of roughly a metre down the middle of the straight course, hence that becomes a slower strip of ground. However, jockeys tend to take their mounts to one rail or the other, so it rarely comes into play.

Drainage: work was carried out in April last year off the course, around one metre behind the rail, due to a 'low spot' at the 5f pole (caused by the heavy rain of winter 2000 making water in that area difficult to shift). The course Vertidrain up the 'running line', generally in the winter, but occasionally in the spring also.

Maximum runners: 5f (24), 6f (24), **7f (Jub)** (17), **7f (rnd)** (17), **1m (Jub)** (20), **1m (rnd)** (18), **1m1f** (20), **1m2f (Jub)** (20), **1m3f30y** (20), **1m4f** (20), **1m6f92y** (14), **2m** (18).

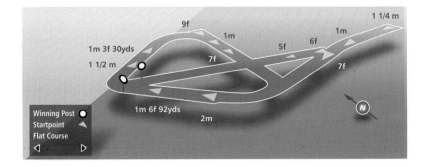

LEICESTER

Stalls: normally go on the stands' rail (low) on the straight course.

Rails: both rails in the straight, which is about 25 metres wide, are permanent.

Straight course points: north-east.

Watering: is done by pop-up sprinklers, but a Briggs boom is now used as well, which helps even out the watering down the middle of the track.

Drainage: the course is on clay, and some minor drainage work was done recently between the 5f and 6f pole to get rid of a wet patch on the stands' side. Vertidraining is done most years in the autumn.

Maximum runners: 5f2y (25), 5f218y (22), 7f9y (20), **1m9y (rnd)** (16), **1m1f218y** (19), **1m3f183y** (22).

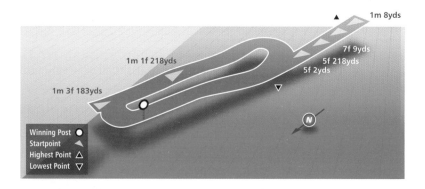

LINGFIELD (TURF)

Stalls: invariably go on the stands' rail (high) for races of between 5f and 7f due to the ground being better that side (they were tried up the far side on a few occasions in 2000). They tend to be positioned down the centre for races over the straight 7f140y.

Rails: during the summer, the option is there to put the stalls away from the stands' side, which reduces the safety factors, by moving the stands' rail by as much as 3 metres inwards, but the far rail is rarely moved.

Straight course points: north.

Watering: a Briggs boom is used, which means there is little wind effect, though sometimes it blows straight down the course.

Drainage: no recent work has been carried out, just routine turf maintenance, but plans are in place for some work to be carried out on the back straight at some point this year.

Maximum runners: 5f (20), 6f (20), 7f (20), 7f140y (18), **1m1f** (14), **1m2f** (16), **1m3f106y** (16), **1m6f** (20), **2m** (20).

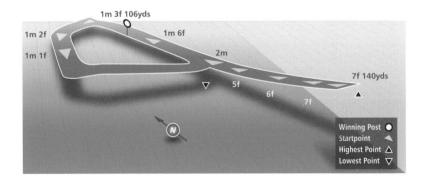

LINGFIELD (ALL-WEATHER)

Stalls: go on the inside (low) for every distance barring 5f and a mile, when they are invariably placed on the stands' rail (high).

Rails: the entire course is 20 metres wide and the rails permanent.

Straight points: north.

Also: the track was re-laid during the summer of last year with a new Polytrack surface, which has proven most popular. This new surface is a massive improvement on the old Equitrack, with much less kickback leading to more competitive and better quality racing.

Maximum runners: **5f** (10), **6f** (14), **7f** (16), **1m** (12), **1m2f** (14), **1m4f** (16), **1m5f** (14), **2m** (14).

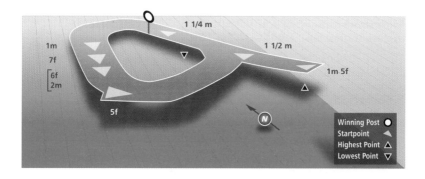

MUSSELBURGH

Stalls: were placed on the stands' side last season, as the far side got a little chewed up during the jumps season. The course used to vary stall positioning (in 1999, for example, they put them up the far side (high) for the first half of the season and on the stands' side for the second half).

Rails: the straight course is about 19 metres wide and the rails are permanent. On the round course there is plenty of scope for stalls' movement, but no set formula.

Sprint course points: west.

Watering: towlines are used for the bends, a Briggs boom for both straights.

Drainage: is rarely a problem, due to the sandy nature of the soil. The only work carried out recently has been some gravel banding near one of the hydrants, and no further work is planned for this year.

Maximum runners: **5f** (17), **7f30y** (14), **1m** (14), **1m1f** (16), **1m4f** (16), **1m5f** (16), **1m6f** (12), **1m7f** (16), **2m** (17).

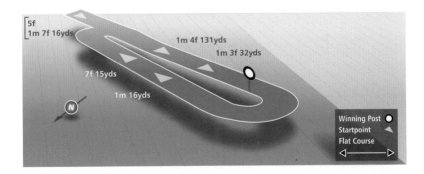

NEWBURY

Stalls: used to go down the centre for important races, but on the stands' side in big-field straight races in order to preserve the ground on the inside for round-course events, but now there's no fixed rule for their positioning.

Rails: the straight course is 32 metres wide at the mile start, tapering down to 18 metres at the finish, and a moveable 'dummy' stands' rail can go out by up to 5 metres for safety reasons (wear and tear).

Straight course points: west.

Watering: the pop-up system used in the 1990s was affected by the prevailing south-westerly wind, but now a Briggs boom is used (which can water the whole track in one day -about 6mm).

Drainage: no major work has been done recently. The 60-metre area that was worked on at the 1m2f point a couple of years ago was so wide on the course that it's rarely raced on.

Maximum runners: 5f34y (25), 6f8y (27), 7f (st) (27), **7f64y (rnd)** (14), 1m (st) (27), **1m7y (rnd)** (14), **1m1f** (18), **1m2f6y** (22), **1m3f5y** (22), **1m4f5y** (22), 1m5f61y (20), **2m** (19).

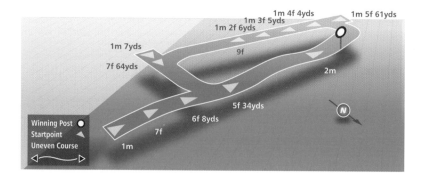

NEWCASTLE

Stalls: go on the stands' side (high) on the straight course, the far side only being employed when absolutely necessary. Flip starts are occasionally used when the ground is especially bad, as was the case once last season.

Rails: the straight course is 21 metres wide and both rails are permanent, but plenty of 'dolling out' occurs during a season.

Straight course points: west.

Watering: an Upton irrigator is used, so the wind has no effect.

Drainage: some work was done late last year on the straight mile between the 6f and mile pole up the far side (under the trees). Also, the trees were cut back 10 metres from the far rail. By the start of this season, Vertidraining will have been done - in both directions on the far side, and just one direction stands side (against the way the horses run) in an attempt to even out the advantage enjoyed by lower-drawn horses that has been apparent in recent years.

Maximum runners: 5f (20), 6f (20), 7f (20), **1m (rnd)** (20), 1m3y (st) (20), **1m1f9y** (20), **1m2f32y** (20), **1m4f93y** (17), **1m6f97y** (14), **2m19y** (20).

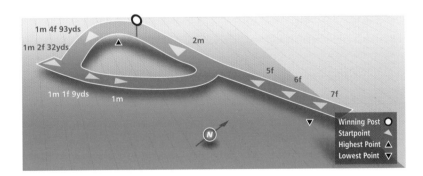

NEWMARKET JULY COURSE

Stalls: are split equally either up the stands' rail (high) and the far rail (the centre is only used in races with small fields (8 or so) when the jockeys are more likely to stay down that part of the track).

Rails: a permanent dividing rail down the centre of the course effectively creates two different tracks, and racing is divided up pretty much equally between the two. All the rails are permanent from the 71/2f point in the straight.

Straight points: south.

Watering: a Briggs boom is used, as well as towlines.

Drainage: no work has been required recently, nor is any planned for the near future.

Maximum runners: 5f (20), 6f (20), 7f (20), 1m (20), **1m2f** (36), **1m4f** (36), **1m6f175y** (36), **2m24y** (36).

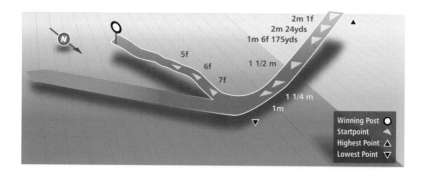

NEWMARKET ROWLEY MILE

Stalls: can go anywhere, centre, far side or stands' side.

Rails: are moveable. A rail can be erected to protect ground when necessary and a 'false' was tried out at both June fixtures and in September 2001, when the far side was brought in by roughly 10 metres. The straight course narrows from being 53 metres wide at the mile start, down to 36 metres at the 5f start.

Straight points: south-east.

Watering: towlines are still mainly used, half a furlong at a time in three parallel lines up to the 3f pole. As the course widens, four parallel lines are used for the reminder of the straight.

Drainage: no work has been required recently, with the track lying on chalk.

Maximum runners: 5f (30), 6f (30), 7f (30), 1m (30), 1m1f (30, Cambs 35), 1m2f (30), **1m4f** (30), **1m6f** (36), **2m** (36), **2m2f** (36).

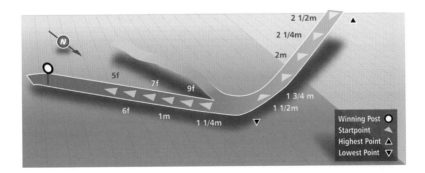

NOTTINGHAM

Stalls: tend to go on the stands' side (high) in sprints, but they can sometimes go on the far side if the stands' rail becomes very wet (in extreme circumstances flip starts have been used).

Rails: the straight course is about 23 metres wide and both rails can be moved. Occasionally, a false inner rail is erected to protect certain parts of the course.

Sprint course points: west.

Watering: an Upton irrigator is used for watering the straight, with towlines employed for the bends.

Drainage: Vertidraining is done annually, and some work was carried out on the 6f chute last winter. Nothing further is planned, but the course is built on a flood plain, so if a low-lying area becomes a problem it will be addressed.

Maximum runners: 5f13y (18), 6f15y (20), **1m54y** (18), **1m1f213y** (16), **1m6f15y** (18), **2m9y** (18), **2m2f18y** (18).

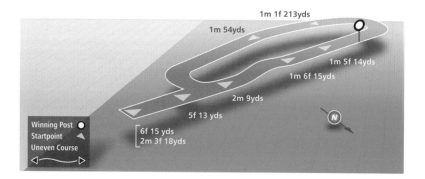

PONTEFRACT

Stalls: go on the inside rail (low) unless the ground becomes soft, when they are sometimes moved to the outside.

Rails: the 5f point is 18 metres wide, and the finishing straight 19.7 metres across. A temporary rail is erected from the 6f pole down to the winning post, 4 metres outside the permanent rail, before the fourth meeting of the season to make use of fresh ground and is taken down before the Friday meeting in mid-July.

Straight points: east.

Watering: an Upton irrigator is used, with towlines in place as a back-up.

Drainage: work is ongoing (the course was built between 1916 and 1918 through a bank, which means there isn't much top soil above the clay). Vertidraining is done twice a year, once in October after the season ends, and once in mid-May before dolling occurs.

Maximum runners: **5f** (18), **6f** (18), **1m4y** (20), **1m2f6y** (19), **1m4f8y** (18), **2m1f22y** (19), **2m1f216y** (19), **2m5f122y** (20).

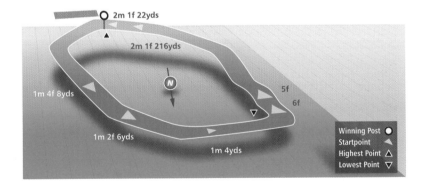

REDCAR

Stalls: go close to the stands' rail (high) the majority of the time, but not right on it because of the shape of the course towards that side.

Rails: the straight course is 30 metres wide at the mile start, narrows down to 25 metres at the 5f point, and both rails can be moved, but rarely are. They were pulled in at the 7f point for the first meeting last year, but then put back immediately.

Straight course points: north.

Watering: pop-up sprinklers are used, and water distribution can be affected by the wind coming from the west.

Drainage: sand-slitting was done before the start of the 2001 season, but nothing major is planned for the near future.

Maximum runners: 5f (23), 6f (26), 7f (29), 1m (30), **1m1f** (16), **1m2f** (17), **1m3f** (16), **1m5f135y** (15), **1m6f19y** (16), **2m4y** (18), **2m3f** (18).

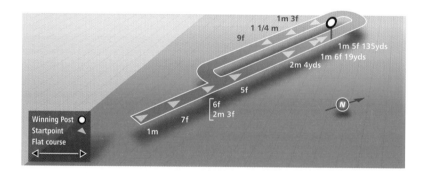

RIPON

Stalls: go on the stands' rail (low) in sprint races, and only change if ground conditions dictate a move (although flip starts are not uncommon here and were used often early last year).

Rails: can be moved, but have not been in the past two seasons. The straight course is about 24 metres wide.

Sprint course points: north.

Watering: pop-up sprinklers were implemented in August '97 in the straight, but the westerly wind, which tends to prevail, blows away from the stands' rail and can make even watering difficult. Consequently, most watering is done during the night when conditions are calmer, but it can also take place throughout the day during particularly dry periods.

Drainage: Vertidraining has taken place before, but was not done last winter.

Maximum runners: 5f (23), 6f (23), **1m** (20), **1m1f** (22), **1m2f** (22), **1m4f60y** (20), **1m6f** (14), **2m** (20), **2m1f203y** (23).

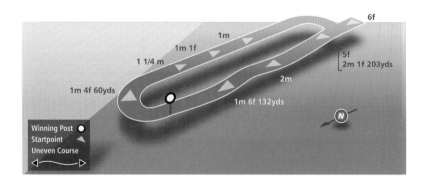

SALISBURY

Stalls: normally go on the far rail (high), except in mid-summer, when a false rail (coming in by up to 4 metres) up that side (for around 5-6 meetings) makes their position more central. On softer ground, the stalls tend to go on the stands' side.

Rails: the straight course widens from being about 19 metres wide at the mile start up to about 29 metres at the 5f point, and the rails are not moved (except in mid-summer).

Straight course points: west.

Watering: towlines and an Upton irrigator are employed, with the former used on the 'loop' and the entrance to the straight.

Drainage: no work has been necessary over the past two seasons, and apparently it's more of a problem retaining water because the course is on chalk.

Maximum runners: 5f (20), 6f (20), 6f212y (20), **1m** (18), **1m2f** (18), **1m4f** (20), **1m6f (flip start)** (20).

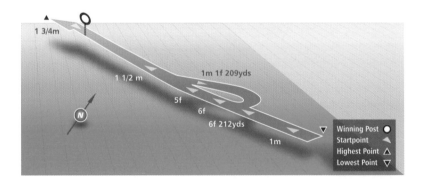

SANDOWN

Stalls: were mostly put up the far side (high) on the sprint chute last year, because apparently the course is less undulating on that side (they used to alternate the position of the stalls between either rail).

Rails: the inside rail on the round course can be moved (as can both rails on the sprint chute, which is about 34 metres wide). Last season, during the summer meetings, the far rail was brought in around 4 metres in order to make use of the fresher ground in the centre of the course.

Sprint chute points: south-west.

Watering: a Briggs boom, towlines and pop-up sprinklers are used, although not so much the latter nowadays.

Drainage: some work was due to be carried out before this season on the 1m2f chute, and a new ditch was to be dug near the stands' side rail to improve drainage alongside the sprint chute.

Maximum runners: 5f6y (20), **7f16y** (16), **1m14y** (18), **1m1f** (16), **1m2f7y** (20), **1m3f91y** (14), **1m6f** (18), **2m78y** (20).

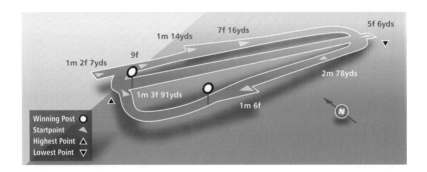

SOUTHWELL (TURF)

Stalls: go in the inside.

Rails: are permanent.

Straight points: south-east.

Watering: a dragline watering system is used here.

Drainage: nothing major has been done, nor is anything planned.

Maximum runners: **6f** (14), **7f** (16), **1m2f** (14), **1m3f** (16), **1m4f** (16), **2m** (16).

SOUTHWELL (ALL-WEATHER)

Stalls: go on the stands' side over the straight 5f (which is about 18 metres wide) but on the inside at every other distance.

Rails: are permanent.

Sprint course points: south-east.

Watering: a 'Bowser' is used.

Also: the entire track was re-laid in October 2000, just three years after it had been done previously.

Maximum runners: **5f** (16), **6f** (16), **7f** (16), **1m** (16), **1m3f** (16), **1m4f** (16), **1m5f** (16), **1m6f** (16), **2m** (16), **2m2f** (16).

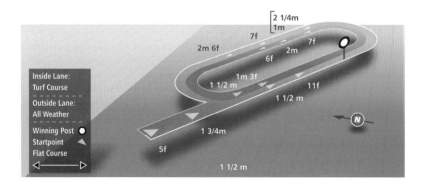

THIRSK

Stalls: go on the stands' side (high) over sprint distances and for races over 1m4f, which start in the straight.

Rails: are both permanent in the straight, which is about 26 metres wide. The running rails round the bends can be moved, and are regularly in order to protect certain areas.

Sprint course points: east.

Watering: used to be done by towlines, which were seriously affected by the prevailing south-westerly wind, but now a Briggs boom is employed, which seemed to have evened things out. The course feels that the bias towards high draws in sprints is still prevalent, but not as strong as it once was.

Drainage: no major work has been done, as the course is sand and gravel-based, and Vertidrained is done each winter.

Maximum runners: 5f (24), 6f (24), **7f** (16), **1m** (18), **1m4f** (19), **2m** (24).

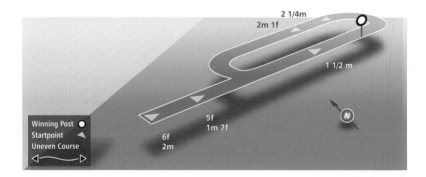

WARWICK

Stalls: go on the inside rail (low) at all distances.

Rails: are permanent, but occasionally a 'false' is erected in the straight. The 5f course starts off about 25 metres wide, but narrows to 14 metres at the bend into the straight.

Sprint course points: north-east.

Watering: is done by an Upton irrigator in the straight, and by towlines on the bends.

Drainage: just Vertidraining each winter.

Maximum runners: 5f (20), 5f110y (20), **6f21y** (17), **7f26y** (20), **1m22y** (20), **1m2f188y** (20), **1m4f134y** (13), **1m6f213y** (14), **1m6f213y** (14), **2m39y** (18), **2m3f13y** (20).

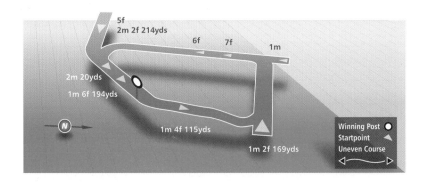

WINDSOR

Stalls: can be positioned anywhere.

Rails: the straight course is 28 metres across at its widest point, but a service road running down to the 6f chute means that maximums have been reduced in the past few years to 25. Early season, the stands' side is dolled off all the way down the straight course (not by a set distance, though).

Sprint course points: east.

Watering: towlines are used, and adjustment can easily be made for any wind effect.

Drainage: work was carried out last November on the crossover and pull-up areas, and the course is regularly slitted. Vertidraining was done for the first time in 2000 on selected areas, and last season the whole course was Vertidrained. No specific plans are afoot for further work.

Maximum runners: **5f10y** (25), **6f** (25), **1m67y** (18), **1m2f7y** (22), **1m3f135y** (20).

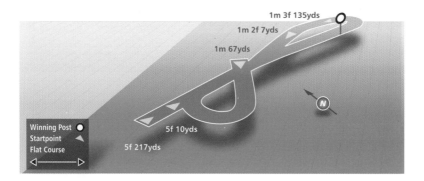

WOLVERHAMPTON ALL-WEATHER

Stalls: usually go on the inside (low) except over 7f (a distance at which amateurs and apprentices do not race) and 1m6f, when they are placed on the outer.

Rails: are permanent.

Straight points: north.

Also: the course was re-laid last July, but seems to ride similarly to before.

Maximum runners: **5f** (13), **6f** (13), **7f** (12), **1m100y** (13), **1m1f79y** (13), **1m4f** (12), **1m6f166y** (12), **2m46y** (13).

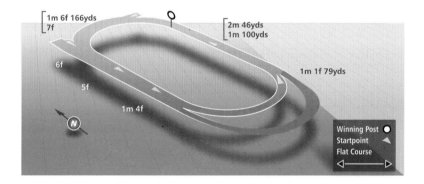

YARMOUTH

Stalls: are rotated, either going on the stands' rail (high) or the far rail (low).

Rails: both rails in the straight, which is 22 metres wide, are permanent and, while they can be dolled out, this rarely happens.

Straight course points: south.

Watering: a Briggs boom was brought in for 1999, replacing the old pop-up sprinklers, and this has been very successful (not affected by the offshore winds) in stopping the old bias towards high numbers.

Drainage: the ground often rides firm due to the course being based on sand, under between 4 and 8 inches of topsoil. However, more meetings were lost than is usual in 2001, due to an unusually high water table. Last winter saw a few small areas attended to and levelled out, but nothing major.

Maximum runners: 5f43y (20), 6f3y (20), 7f3y (20), 1m3y (20), **1m2f21y** (17), **1m3f101y** (17), **1m6f17y** (20), **2m** (20), **2m2f51y** (20).

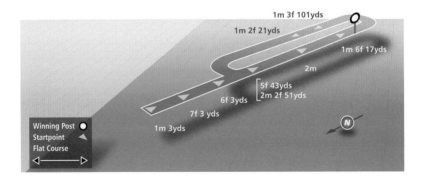

YORK

Stalls: usually go on the inside (low), although there have been cases of them going on the outside rail over 6f214y. This year, the sprint capacity is being reduced from 23 to 21 due to safety reasons.

Rails: both rails in the straight are permanent, but a 'false' can be used in the later stages of the season in order to preserve the ground. The course is about 34 metres wide for the first quarter-mile on the 6f214y chute, 24-25 metres wide at the 6f start, narrowing down to 20 metres at finish.

Sprint course points: north.

Watering: pop-up sprinklers are used to cover both sides of the straight. The prevailing wind is a westerly, and watering is always done in the night when conditions are usually calmer.

Drainage: little work has been done recently, although two years ago some was carried out at the 7f point underneath the wood.

Maximum runners: 5f (21), 6f (21), **6f214y** (24), **7f202y** (26), **1m205y** (27), **1m2f85y** (22), **1m3f195y** (22), **1m5f194y** (22), **1m7f195y** (22).

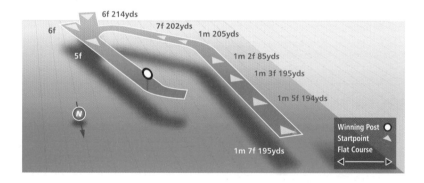

CHAPTER 3

Trend Horses

Andrew Mount

In my experience, a large number of supposed shock results are explicable by a closer analysis of a horse's ideal requirements, by studying past career form and identifying the circumstances under which a horse has run well.

Distance and going preferences are an obvious starting point; Taras Emperor, for example, is unbeaten in three 5f starts on heavy ground. However, the ideal requirements of most racehorses tend to be rather more complicated than this.

Noticeable preferences may include one or more of the following: the need for a small or large field, for a recent outing / long absence between races, for a draw next to a rail, for a certain class of race, for a flat or an undulating course, for only a short trip to the racecourse.

Many sprinters labelled 'dodgepots' often just have very specific require-ments, a set of conditions that may only be found once or twice in a season (or not at all!).

This section includes around 100 such horses (including all runs up to and including Tuesday, 2 April), and I'm certain a profit will be made from backing them under their right conditions this season.

Just for the record, here are some hand-picked non-sprinters, for those who don't mind watching their races for longer than 70 seconds:

KAIAPOI (fast ground, Chester).

MELODIAN (7f-1m, soft ground, local course).

PULAU PINANG (1m2f-1m5f, fast ground, not seasonal debut).

SMOKEY FROM CAPLAW (fresh);

SPORTING GESTURE (small field).

TURNED OUT WELL (Beverley, fresh).

TURNPOLE (fast ground, small field);

TURTLE VALLEY (1m6f, soft ground).

WAVE OF OPTIMISM (2m, soft ground, right-hand course, fresh).

WEET FOR ME (small field).

Abbajabba did best of those drawn low in the Great St Wilfrid

ABBAJABBA

Distance: 5f (0-7); 6f (4-22); 7f (0-2).
Going: G-F+ (0-8); Good (2-9); G-S (1-6); Soft (0-4); Hvy (1-3); AWT (0-1).

Combine 6f with good or softer ground and his record becomes: 25066311104529310 (4-17). Knock out runs pre-2000 under these conditions and his figures become worthy of still closer inspection: 3rd – outlier at Nottingham (first six drawn 10, 1, 17, 8, 4 and 3 of 20), 1st, 1st, 1st, 0 – poorly drawn at Salisbury in stall 1 of 17 (trainer thought race may have come too soon (only four days after his previous start)), 4th – of 22, 5th – '01 seasonal debut, 2nd – of 18, 9th – of 29 (fifth home of his group (hampered)), 3rd – outlier in Great St Wilfrid at Ripon after a 105-day break (first four drawn 17, 23, 1 and 14 of 23), 1st and 11th. Although he was beaten on his debut last season, he goes well fresh, particularly judging by his Nottingham reappearance in 2000, when first home up the stands' side (Tony Culhane, second home on that side on Sharp Hat, subsequently told David Chapman the rail was riding like 'a swamp'). Pay particular attention when he's drawn next to a rail.

ALPEN WOLF (IRE)

Distance: 5f (1-11); 6f (6-37); 7f (2-16).
Going: Firm (2-4); G-F (6-30); Good (1-13); G-S (0-2); Soft– (0-4); AWT (1-11).
Fresh (seasonal debut): (0-4).
Field size: 15+ (0-24); 14- (10-40).
Headgear: visor (0-3); blinkers (0-1).

Combine a small field (14 runners or fewer) with good to firm or faster ground, no headgear, any distance, and not making his seasonal reappearance, and his record becomes: 5811111332517211328 (8-19) (he's finished in the first three in 15 of his last 18 starts under these conditions). Both 7f wins came on turning tracks (Epsom and Warwick) in slowly-run races and he's probably best suited by shorter, and while he's won on officially good ground, the time taken that day suggested it was good to firm (with him breaking standard time by 1.5secs). A winner off 85 in the past, he's now down into the mid-60s on Turf and showed some form off that sort of mark on the All-Weather over the winter, including when second off 64 in a 0-70 Classified Stakes on 11 February.

Andreyev (right) should do well for Jim Goldie

ANDREYEV (IRE)

Distance: 5f (1-10); 6f (7-35); 7f (2-8).
Going: G-F+ (1-11); Good (5-19); G-S (1-10); Soft (2-8); Hvy (1-3); AWT (0-1).
Fresh (first two runs of the season or after break of six weeks+): (6-16).
Field size: 14+ (0-12); 13- (10-41).
Overseas form: (1-7).

Combine 6f in the UK, good or softer ground in fields of 13 or fewer with being fresh, and his record becomes: 1104116 (4-7). A career-low rating means he can now get into handicaps and carrying weight seems no problem. His first two runs at a time when the stable was quiet, can be ignored.

ANNIJAZ

Distance: 6f (0-5); 7f (3-22); 1m (0-10); 1m1f+ (0-6).
Going: G-S+ (2-23); Soft / Heavy (0-5); AWT (1-15).

Combine 7f with good to soft or faster turf and her record becomes: 22301732136 (2-11). While two from 11 isn't an impressive strike-rate, there were excuses for most of the defeats; from left to right: 2nd – ran green on second career start, 2nd – beaten 0.75l in a 20-runner Newmarket seller (needed the race after a three-month absence), 4th – outlier at Salisbury (first six drawn 12, 17, 20, 2, 18 and 14 of 20), 3rd – outlier at Lingfield (first three drawn 14, 12 and 6 of 14), 0 – making good headway when badly hampered, 1st, 7th – poorly drawn at Yarmouth but finished third of the low numbers, 3rd – wasted a high draw by racing down the unfavoured centre at Lingfield, 2nd – beaten a short-head in 17-runner Epsom handicap, 1st, 3rd – poorly drawn at Lingfield, and 4th – making headway when hampered. Given her excellent record at Epsom (a win and a short-head second from two starts) it was disappointing she didn't run there last season, but she's recently joined Milton Bradley, who'll find the right races (she's already won for him on the All-Weather). She may even prove effective at 6f in a big field.

ANTHONY MON AMOUR (USA)

Distance: 5f (3-24); 6f (2-16); 7f+ (0-3).
Going: Firm (0-4); G-F (3-10); Good (1-13); G-S (0-10); AWT (1-6).
Field size: 13+ (1-27); 12- (4-16).

Combine 5f (both 6f wins came when making all in small-field juvenile events) with good to firm or faster ground and a small field (12 or fewer) and his record becomes: 153261 (2-6). He starts the season on a mark of 59, the rating off which he secured his latest win at Newcastle last July.

AUTUMNAL (IRE)

Distance: 5f (2-6); 6f (1-6); 7f+ (0-4).
Going: Good+ (2-8); G-S (1-6); Soft / Heavy (0-2).
Class: A (0-11); B- (3-5).

Combine 5f-6f with good to soft or faster ground and running in Class B company or lower, and her record becomes: 3111 (3-4), the only defeat coming when running green on her racecourse debut at two.

Autumnal (left) is three from four in Class B company on decent ground

BABY BARRY

Distance: 5f (1-12); 6f (3-18); 7f (0-7).
Going: Firm (0-4); G-F (1-7); Good (3-12); G-S (0-5); Soft– (0-7); AWT (0-2).
Course: flat (1-19); undulating (3-18).

Headgear: blinkers (1-3); visor (3-9); none (0-25).
Basically, he is ineffective over 5f and on flat courses with his only success under these conditions coming in a Class F maiden at two. Combine 6f on good or faster ground with the wearing of headgear and an undulating course, and his record becomes: 13114 (3-5). From left to right: 1st, 3rd – raced on the other side of the track to the winner (losing out by only a head on his flank), 1st, 1st, and 4th – in a 28-runner handicap, when the going was softer than the official good. He starts the season rated 75 (he has been up to 85), and hopefully he'll come down a bit further by being campaigned on unsuitable courses / without headgear.

BALI ROYAL

Distance: 5f (5-15); 6f (1-5).
Going: Firm (1-2); G-F (1-4); Good (2-4); G-S (1-4); Soft– (0-4); AWT (1-2).
Fresh (after break of six weeks+): (0-4); six weeks or less (6-16).

Combine 5f with good to soft or faster ground and a return to action within six weeks, and her record becomes: 12113121 (5-8), with the three defeats excusable. From left to right: 2nd – did best of the low numbers at Windsor (first three drawn 17, 7 and 14 of 15), 3rd – beaten 0.5l at Chepstow (poorly drawn in 3, first two drawn high), and 2nd – to the useful Indian Prince.

BANJO BAY

Distance: 5f (0-4); 6f (1-3); 7f (1-4); 1m (0-3).
Going: G-F (0-4); Good (1-5); G-S (1-3); Soft (0-2).

Despite winning at 7f, and running well for along way in the Lincoln, he looks a better and less-exposed horse at 6f, his three career starts at that trip having seen him win his maiden at Pontefract (on good to soft), finish a close second in the Great St Wilfrid at Ripon (on good) and come fifth in the Ayr Gold Cup on unsuitably fast ground (doing best of the three-year-olds). He has occasionally shown a tendency to start slowly, which will need sorting, but that aside, a campaign geared around the big 6f handicaps would seem the soundest option.

BAYONET

Distance: 5f (0-4); 6f (1-17); 7f (0-6).
Going: Firm (0-2); G-F (1-13); Good (0-9); G-S (0-2); AWT (0-1).

At first glance, her overall profile doesn't look particularly appealing, but going through her 6f runs in detail, there are a lot of valid excuses hidden within her form. It's a fair bet that she doesn't truly stay 7f, but she has finished placed at Chepstow and Lingfield on her last two starts at that distance (both courses have significant downhill sections which bring out the best in her). Check out her overall record at the two courses (on good to firm or faster ground, without blinkers): 41222 (1-5). She starts this season well handicapped and will probably come down further yet from her mark of 54, as she usually needs a couple of runs and has looked a summer mare the past two years. The chances are she'll show signs of coming back to form before winning – as when running a storming race towards the centre at Salisbury late last June – and she could well run up a sequence on fast ground, granted better luck with the draw.

BEAUCHAMP PILOT

Distance: 5f (0-1); 6f (0-1); 7f (1-2); 1m (2-2); 1m1f+ (0-1).
Going: G-F (0-2); Good (1-2); G-S (1-1); Soft (1-1); AWT (0-1).
Course: straight (3-5); round (0-2).

With only seven career starts to his name, it's hard to make any concrete judgments about ideal requirements, but the way he improved last season when handed a trip of 7f or a mile on a straight track, with cut in the ground, would suggest that these are the conditions under which to back him. His only defeat under them, over 7f at Folkestone, probably came as a result of his jockey making too much use of him, and races like the Victoria Cup and Royal Hunt Cup look tailor-made this season. Ascot clearly suits, judging by his win from a difficult draw (also ran well from a poor draw over 5f at Beverley previously) there last September (next two home from low draws won their next starts).

BECKY SIMMONS

Distance: 5f (1-1); 6f (3-7); 7f (0-4).
Going: G-F+ (2-4); Good (2-6); G-S (0-1); AWT (0-1).
Fresh (first two runs of the season or after break of six weeks+): (3-5).

Combine 5f-6f with good or faster ground when fresh and her record becomes a hard-to-fault: 111 (3-3).

BEYOND CALCULATION (USA)

Distance: 5f (1-18); 6f (8-45); 7f (0-5).
Going: Firm (3-7); G-F (4-25); Good (1-15); G-S (1-12); Soft– (0-3); AWT (0-6).
Fresh (absence since last run): 18 days+ (0-21); 17- (9-47).

Combine 6f with good to firm or faster ground and an absence of 17 days or fewer and his record becomes: 18750621211140421 (6-17). Interestingly, the six wins were all preceded by a win or a placed effort, and adding that proviso to the above criteria leaves his figures as: 1121111 (6-7). Hopefully, a few early-season sighters will have him back to a mark in the low 70s (his last win came off 72).

BEYOND THE CLOUDS (IRE)

Distance: 5f (5-22); 6f (0-6); 7f+ (0-4).
Going: G-F (2-14); Good (3-7); G-S (0-3); Soft / Heavy (0-7); AWT (0-1).
Headgear: visor (0-5).

Combine 5f with good or faster ground and no headgear and his record becomes: 1414219113804 (5-13). While his record on good going looks excellent at first glance, a closer analysis reveals a different story, as for each of his three wins on it the *Raceform* going allowance suggested ground of good to firm or faster. Indeed, he broke the course record at Windsor, while at Beverley, both this race and the other 5f event on the card were run at below standard time. Count these three runs as having come on good to firm, and his career record at 5f on fast without headgear would become: 14142191138 (5-11), including a Windsor record of: 121. A right-hand rail clearly helps him.

BLACKHEATH (IRE)

Distance: 5f (0-2); 6f (1-18); 7f (0-3).
Going: Firm (0-1); G-F (0-10); Good (1-8); G-S (0-3); Soft (0-1).
Fresh: first run of year (0-4); second (0-3); third (1-3); fourth run+ (0-13).

He has always at best fresh in the past, but that may change for David Nicholls this year. Last on his comeback at Doncaster, he is now down to a career-low rating and should be watched on decent ground at 6f when he finally shows form.

BLAKESHALL BOY

Distance: 5f (4-21); 6f (0-12).
Going: Good+ (4-23); G-S- (0-10).
Fresh (absence since last run): 16 days+ (0-8); 8-15 (1-16); 7- (3-9).
Field size: 20+ (0-10); 12-19 (2-11); 11- (2-12).

Combine 5f with good or faster ground and a field of fewer than 20 runners, when racing within seven days of his previous run, and his record becomes: 1511 (3-4). The fifth can be excused on account of an unfavourable low draw at Beverley, and he starts this season on a rating of 75, 4lb below his last winning mark.

BOLD KING

Distance: 6f (0-3); 7f (2-20); 1m (2-13); 1m1f+ (0-2).
Going: Firm (0-1); G-F (0-8); Good (1-19); G-S (1-4); Soft (1-4); AWT (1-2).
Fresh (after break of six weeks+): (3-9); less than six weeks (1-29).

Combine 7f-1m with good or softer ground (or Southwell Fibresand) when fresh, and his record becomes: 1621120 (3-7). Restricting this to runs at 7f only, his record is: 110 (2-3). His two wins at a mile both came in slowly-run, small-field races and, in larger fields with the emphasis more on stamina, he doesn't truly stay. Watch for him first time this season, especially over 7f if the ground is slow, probably in a handicap, now that he's down to a three-season low rating of 84.

BOND BOY

Distance: 5f (4-13); 6f (0-9).
Going: G-F (0-2); Good (2-10); G-S (0-2); Soft (2-5); Heavy (0-3).
Fresh (first two runs of the season or after break of five weeks+): (1-10).

Combine 5f with good or softer ground and knock out his runs when fresh, and his record becomes: 2731181 (3-7). His only 'fresh' win came when returned 11-10 favourite for a poor Beverley maiden (scraped home from a 33-1 shot).

BOWLERS BOY

Distance: 5f (5-38); 6f (5-43); 7f+ (0-2).
Going: G-F+ (2-18); Good (2-29); G-S (1-15); Soft (3-12); Hvy (2-8); AWT (0-1).
Fresh (absence since last run): 29 days+ (0-16); 22-28 (1-5); 15-21 (2-15); 8-14 (0-26); 7- (7-21).
Course: stiff finish (8-48); other (2-35).

Combine 5f-6f with a very recent run (seven days or less) and a track with a stiff finish (ie, Hamilton, Newcastle, Pontefract) and his record becomes: 222201010121413 (5-15). Splitting these 15 runs into ground and class categories reveals some even more interesting patterns:

Going: G-F+ (1-7); G-S- (4-8).
Class: D+ (1-6); E- (4-9).

Combining Class E or lower with good to soft ground or worse, his record becomes: 211213 (3-6). The three defeats all came at 5f (he's looked happier at six as he's got older), and it's worth noting that, while he has won after more than seven days off, he hasn't done so since '97 (no wins on fast ground since '96). Some feel he's best in the autumn, but that's not true – he just needs his conditions and a fair mark; the 59 he starts this season on is just that.

Brevity (No. 3) has improved hugely for Milton Bradley

BREVITY

Distance: 5f (0-7); 6f (8-24); 7f+ (1-13).
Going: Firm (3-4); G-F (5-15); Good (1-9); G-S (0-2); Soft– (0-7); AWT (0-7).

Combine 6f with good to firm or faster ground and his record becomes: 701111101102 (7-12). Looking at his runs for Milton Bradley only, this becomes even better: 1111101102 (7-10), with all three defeats excusable on account of the draw (at Newcastle, York and Ayr). His only win at 7f+ came when he was returned 4-6 for a small-field handicap at Brighton on firm, almost hard, ground. His trainer didn't seem to mind running him on soft last year to get him fit, and don't be surprised to see a repetition to get him down a few pounds from 101.

CANDLERIGGS (IRE)

Distance: 5f (0-5); 6f (2-13); 7f (0-1).
Going: G-F (0-7); Good (2-6); G-S (0-3); Soft (0-3).
Fresh (first two runs or after break of six weeks+): (2-9); others: (0-10).

Combine 6f with good or softer ground, when fresh, and his record becomes: 5161 (2-4). He was poorly berthed in stall 12 when fifth at York (first three drawn 6, 7 and 3 of 15), although there was no obvious excuse for the other defeat.

CHURCH MICE (IRE)

Distance: 5f (1-4); 6f (2-10); 7f (0-7).
Going: G-F+ (1-4); Good (0-3); G-S (0-3); Soft (1-5); Hvy (1-2); AWT (0-4).
Course: straight (3-13); round (0-8); stiff finish (2-7); easy finish (1-14).

Concentrate solely on runs at a straight track with a stiff finish (or any finish on heavy) and her record becomes: 1121523 (3-7). Her three most recent defeats under these conditions came in Class C events, representing a clear class divide, because at Class D or lower her record is: 1121 (3-4), the only defeat coming when an outlier at Doncaster (raced far side when the action was down the centre). She's been beaten 13l, 28l, 6l and 4l on her last four starts round a bend. Despite her form not tailing off completely last backend, she's been generously dropped to 76 (1lb lower than the mark off which she won at Newcastle) having finished second to Hot Tin Roof (on impossible terms) when officially rated 83.

COLD CLIMATE

Distance: 5f (0-6); 6f (3-20); 7f+ (0-6).
Going: G-F (2-12); Good (1-10); G-S (0-5); Soft (0-2); Heavy (0-3).
Headgear: visor (0-5).

Combine 6f with good or faster ground and no headgear while under the charge of Bob Jones (he was 0-3 for Roger Charlton) and his record becomes: 028313012106 (3-12). On good to firm or faster ground, this improves to: 28311 (2-5), with the three defeats excusable. From left to right: 2nd – Windsor outlier (first four drawn 21, 1, 18 and 20 of 22), 8th – poorly drawn on the outside of the field at Doncaster, 3rd – making good progress when badly hampered at Epsom, 1st and 1st. His trainer was convinced in the past that cut in the ground was essential, and he may still prove as effective on soft – he's still improving.

COLLEGE MAID (IRE)

Distance: 5f (4-35); 6f (2-23); 7f (0-5).
Going: Firm (0-6); G-F (1-12); Good (3-12); G-S (1-13); Soft (0-12); Hvy (1-8).
Fresh (absence since last run): 6 days+ (1-48); 3-5 (3-9); 1-2 (2-6).

Combine good or softer ground with a break of five days or fewer, and her record becomes: 11515013210 (5-11). From left to right: 1st, 1st, 5th –

Class E 6f handicap, ground a shade too fast, 1st, 5th – Class D 5f handicap, probably unsuited by the long journey (250 miles+), 0 – 12th in the Ayr Silver Cup, 1st, 3rd – Class C 6f handicap, 2nd – Class D 6f handicap, doing well from her draw, 1st, and 0 – 13th in the Ayr Silver Cup. With her handicap mark now down to 69 from 76 (she's won off 67), she should find numerous opportunities to add to her tally, especially at 5f with cut in the ground (her sole good to firm win came by a short-head in a Class F maiden at two).

CONNECT

Distance: 5f (3-20); 6f (0-5); 7f+ (0-3).
Going: Firm (0-1); G-F (2-13); Good (1-7); G-S (0-3); AWT (0-4).
Field size: 12+ (0-19); 11- (3-9).
Headgear: visor (0-2); blinkers (0-2).

Combine a small field (11 runners or fewer) with an easy 5f and no headgear and his record becomes: 2111 (3-4), the defeat coming by a short-head on his debut. He is 2-3 at Yarmouth, the only defeat coming when ridden like a questionable stayer over 6f, and he starts the season on 82 (2lb above his last winning mark).

Damalis (No 3) has won 4 from 6 over 5f at Chester, with valid excuses the other twice

DAMALIS (IRE)

Distance: 5f (6-29); 6f (0-14).
Going: Firm (0-1); G-F (3-15); Good (1-11); G-S (0-6); Soft (2-9); Hvy (0-1).

Despite having two wins to her name on soft, they came in a weak Ripon juvenile conditions event and when making all up the favoured far rail at Sandown. She is almost certainly better on faster ground and at Chester.

Chester: 134113132 (4-9); others (2-33, including 24 consecutive defeats).

Her record solely in 5f events around Chester is even more impressive: 141113 (4-6) and, while there was no obvious excuse for the fourth, the other defeat can be forgiven on account of her being drawn widest of all in stall 12 behind Danehurst (first five drawn 5, 2, 12, 3 and 1 of 11). She also overcame stall 8 to win a 0-100 handicap last May, making her the first horse to win a 5f Chester handicap from higher than the 6 box in several seasons.

DANCING MYSTERY

Distance: 5f (14-71); 6f (1-15).
Going: G-F+ (6-30); Good (1-22); G-S (2-11); Soft / Heavy (3-11); AWT (3-12).

Most of his fast-ground wins have come at Class D or below, so the above figures don't really paint a true picture as, given that he's been placed in Group 2 company, he's unlikely to run at such a low level again for a long time. Consequently, his runs in Class C or higher company offer a better guide:

Class C+: G-F+ (1-8); Good (0-8); G-S (1-4); Soft (3-5); Heavy (0-1); AWT (0-5).

Combine 5f with good to soft or softer ground and at Class C or above and his record becomes: 1211502142 (4-10). Three of these defeats can be excused; from left to right: 2nd – a clear outlier at Ascot (first eight drawn 17, 7, 14, 12, 13, 18, 10 and 19 of 19), 5th – a clear outlier at Doncaster (first six drawn 14, 12, 13, 15, 3 and 16 of 17), and 0 – ground faster than good to soft, as indicated by a 'minus' *Raceform* going allowance. He'll be worth following again this autumn.

DANEHURST

Distance: 5f (4-7); 6f (2-2).
Going: G-F (2-2); Good (0-1); G-S (1-2); Soft (2-2); Hvy (0-1); AWT (1-1).
UK form: (6-7); *Overseas form:* (0-2).

Her only poor run in the UK came on her seasonal debut last year, although facing fit rivals and finishing ninth in the Group 2 King's Stand was no disgrace. Her two worst runs have been in Ireland and France; she may be a poor traveller but, if the improvement continues, she'll finish up champion sprinter this time.

Danehurst looks set to become champion sprinter, but beware when she travels abroad

DEEP BLUE

Distance: 5f (0-5); 6f (1-3); 7f (1-7); 1m (0-1).
Going: G-F (0-2); Good (1-6); G-S (0-2); Soft (0-3); Hvy (1-1); AWT (0-2).
Fresh (after break of six weeks+): (2-5).

Combine 6f-7f with good or softer ground, when fresh and his record becomes: 11 (2-2), the wins coming at 4-1 and 25-1. Pay close attention to him first time up again this year, as he could well come in under-rated once more, and his rating is now just 65, 10lb lower than that off which he made his '01 Turf comeback. According to his trainer, Jon Scargill, he'll be ready to go quite early.

EASTERN TRUMPETER

Distance: 5f (13-58); 6f (0-6).
Going: G-F (1-18); Good (3-9); G-S (2-6); Soft (1-8); Hvy (1-5); AWT (5-18).

In the last two seasons his 5f form on good or good to soft ground reads: 011111520 (5-9), the defeats being, from left to right: 0 – poorly drawn at Bath, a track that possibly didn't suit, 5th – raced on the unfavoured stands' side at Salisbury, 2nd – beaten in a photo at York, and 0 – returning from an eight-week layoff and clearly in need of the race. The fact that he was still competitive on fast ground off marks around 88 late last year would make one feel that a season-starting figure of 85 shouldn't be an off-putter. He has an excellent record at York, having registered two wins and a second in three starts and, granted dead ground, will be of particular interest if returned there this season.

EFFERVESCE (IRE)

Distance: 5f (1-11); 6f (1-6); 7f (0-2).
Going: G-F (0-3); Good (0-5); G-S (1-6); Soft (0-3); AWT (1-2).
Field size: 14+ (0-6); 13- (2-13).

With only two successes from 18 starts, she wouldn't look an obvious horse to follow, but (from admittedly limited evidence) she has shown some strong preferences. According to her trainer, she needs cut in the ground, but she certainly handles good to firm, only going down by a neck at Newmarket on fast ground behind Blakeshall Boy (who was facing his ideal conditions). Combine 5f-6f with a smallish field (13 runners or fewer) and her record becomes: 468129203381 (2-12), with several of the unplaced efforts forgivable. From left to right: 4th – on her racecourse debut, 6th – failed to handle Pontefract, hanging right throughout, 8th – raced too freely, 9th – an outclassed 50-1 shot in Listed company, 0 – badly hampered, 3rd – an outlier at Thirsk last August (first four drawn 11, 9, 1 and 12 of 12), and 8th – poorly drawn at Ripon. She won on her All-Weather debut at Southwell in February and is definitely worth watching back on Turf.

FANTASY BELIEVER

Distance: 5f (2-12); 6f (4-14).
Going: G-S+ (5-19); Soft / Heavy (1-7).
Fresh (absence since last run): 15 days+ (1-12); 14- (5-14).

Combine 6f with a recent run and his record becomes: 45141151 (4-8), with two of the defeats attributable to being too early in the season (he seems to take a while to reach peak-fitness):
First run of the season: 37 (0-2); second run: 24 (0-2); third run: 45 (0-2).
Combine 6f with a recent run and starting for the fourth time of the year or later and we are left with: 141151 (4-6). He went up 19lb in the weights last year and may need a few runs to achieve peak fitness and to come down a few pounds.

FLAK JACKET

Distance: 5f (2-21); 6f (5-16); 7f (0-4).
Going: G-F (3-13); Good (2-10); G-S (0-8); Soft (1-7); Heavy (1-3).
Month: Mar-May (0-10); June (1-4); July (4-9); Aug (2-8); Sept-Oct (0-10).

Combine 5f-6f with running between June and August and his record becomes: 119022111302412410 (7-18). Looking at 6f only in June, July or

August, this improves to: 11902110210 (5-11). Looking solely at runs within five days or his previous start, this is further enhanced to: 11121 (4-5). He starts this season on 68, 1lb lower than the mark he kicked off on last year (has won off 80 in the past).

FRIAR TUCK

Distance: 5f (1-10); 6f (4-35); 7f+ (0-4).
Going: Firm (2-5); G-F (2-14); Good (0-14); G-S (0-5); Soft (1-7); Heavy (0-4).
Fresh (first two runs of the season or after break of six weeks+): (1-13).
Field size: 12+ (2-35); 11- (3-14).

Combine a small field (11 runners or fewer) with good to firm or faster ground and 5f-6f and his record becomes: 1342112 (3-7). He starts the year well handicapped on 71, given that his comeback second last season was achieved off 78 and that his following close-up sixth (over 5f, which looked a touch sharp) at Haydock came off 82.

GDANSK (IRE)

Distance: 5f (5-24) 6f (0-7); 7f+ (0-3).
Going: G-F (0-7); Good (0-9); G-S (2-6); Soft (1-7); Heavy (2-5).

Combine 5f with good to soft or softer ground and his record becomes: 14101121068 (5-11). From left to right: 1st, 4th – good run from stall 12 in a Chester handicap, 1st, 0 – never looked happy at Ayr, hanging most of the way, 1st, 1st, 2nd – beaten 1l by well-handicapped Pipadash in a Haydock handicap, 1st, 0 – outclassed in a Class B Ascot handicap, 6th – beaten less than 2l after losing ground at the start, and 8th – looked to have had enough in a Windsor handicap. His form has tailed off in October the last two seasons, so be wary of backing him in the autumn, and his Ayr record is poor as well, with him having finished 16th, 8th, 15th, 13th and 8th in five starts (some admittedly at 6f). He has, though, shown himself capable of going well fresh, winning his first two starts last year, and he starts the season on a fair mark.

GENIAL GENIE

Distance: 5f (1-1); 6f (1-4); 7f (2-14); 1m (0-4); 1m1f+ (0-2).
Going: Firm (1-2); G-F (1-5); Good (1-5); Soft (0-4); AWT (1-9).

Within a ten-week period last season he ran over trips ranging from 5f to 1m2f, but is clearly best at 7f or shorter, and he remains unexposed at sprint distances. Combine 5f-7f with good or faster ground and his record becomes: 321410122 (3-9). From left to right: 3rd – hampered twice in 7f Thirsk handicap (sent off 20-1), yet only beaten around 1l, 2nd – beaten a head in a 6f Ripon maiden handicap, 1st – won a 6f Thirsk maiden handicap despite a low draw, 4th – of 25 in a 6f Redcar handicap, racing on the opposite side to the winner and only being beaten two necks in the far-side group, 1st – won a 5f Pontefract handicap on his only career start at the distance, 0 – tenth of 20 in a 6f Redcar handicap, *Raceform*'s race-reader noting he was 'not disgraced from what turned out to be a modest draw', 1st, 2nd – in a Beverley handicap, where the 7f100y on rain-softened ground was against him, and 2nd – beaten a short-head in a 7f Catterick handicap. He's been tried at and beaten over a mile on the All-Weather since winning over 7f at Southwell in November, and hopefully the Handicapper will cut him some slack before he returns to shorter on Turf.

GET STUCK IN (IRE)

Distance: 5f (1-28); 6f (3-26); 7f (0-1).
Going: Firm (0-4); G-F (0-12); Good (2-18); G-S (0-6); Soft (1-13); Hvy (1-2).
Course: stiff finish (1-16), easy finish (3-39).

His only win on a course with a stiff finish came at Hamilton in an amateur event back in June '99; combine 5f-6f with good to soft or softer ground on a course with an easy finish and his record becomes: 2207123031242 (2-13). He's spent much of his career on marks in the mid 80s (currently 84) and may need to come down to 80 or below to win again. He has an excellent record at Ripon (one win and two seconds (in photo finishes)), so the Great St Wilfrid would look an ideal target this season, and never cross him off if he's a borderline case when it comes to the draw; his mid-race pace often overcomes this.

GOODENOUGH MOVER

Distance: 6f (1-3); 7f (2-10); over 7f (1-11).
Going: Good+ (4-19); G-S- (0-5).
Course: straight (4-14); round (0-10).

His only win at further than 7f came when returned 13-8 favourite for a slowly-run, small-field event (allowed an uncontested lead) and he doesn't look to stay beyond that distance. Combine good or faster ground with a straight track, and his record since joining Jeff King (0-6 for previous handler) is: 111149008 (4-9). At 7f only this becomes: 11490 (2-5), with all the defeats excusable. From left to right: 4th – involved in protracted duel for the lead, 9th – poorly drawn (finishing second in his group), and 0 – went off too fast under an apprentice. A quiet '01 sees him very handily weighted on 63, 7lb below his last winning mark.

GORETSKI (IRE)

Distance: 5f (17-98); 6f (2-17).
Month: Jan-May (2-43); June (4-11); July (4-11); Aug (6-13); Sept+ (3-37).

Look only at his runs over 5f in June, July or August ('97 onwards) and his record becomes: 1111211051121185113453802160 (13-28). Concentrating on August this improves to: 1211132160 (5-10). He remains must-bet material when the ground comes up soft during the summer.

HARMONIC WAY

Distance: 5f (0-2); 6f (5-32); 7f (0-6).
Going: Firm (0-3); G-F (5-15); Good (0-12); G-S (0-2); Soft (0-6); Heavy (0-2).
Field size: 16+ (4-15); 15- (1-25).

His only win in a field of fewer than 16 came when favourite for a Salisbury maiden on his two-year-old debut; combine 6f with good to firm or faster ground and a big field (16 or more) and his record becomes: 21111 (4-5), including wins at 12-1, 12-1, 13-2 and 10-1. He was due to be packed off to stud in Greece at the end of '00, but thankfully wasn't, as he's still improving. The July Cup will again offer his best chance of a Group 1, granted fast ground and a high draw (he's happy coming through a gap up a rail, as shown at Windsor and Ascot).

Harmonic Way has an outstanding record on fast ground in big fields

HENRY HALL (IRE)

Distance: 5f (6-42); 6f (0-2).
Going: Firm (1-2); G-F (2-20); Good (3-13); G-S (0-5); Soft (0-4).
Class: A (0-7); B (1-23); C (2-9); D (2-3); E (0-1); F (1-1).

Combine 5f with good (which seems ideal) or faster ground and Class C or lower company and his record becomes: 1231127231401 (5-13)..

HILLTOP WARNING

Distance: 6f (0-5); 7f (4-10); 1m+ (0-1).
Going: G-F (4-9); Good (0-3); G-S (0-2); Soft (0-1); AWT (0-1).
Fresh (after break of six weeks+): (3-6).

Combine 7f with good to firm or faster ground and a break of six weeks or longer and his record becomes: 111 (3-3). He twice managed to win from a very difficult draw (6 of 17 over 7f at Goodwood and up the stands' rail at Yarmouth at the one meeting where that side rode way slower) and there should be more to come.

INDIAN BAZAAR (IRE)

Distance: 5f (5-20); 6f+ (0-7).
Going: Good+ (5-21); G-S- (0-6).
Fresh (absence since last run): 15 days+ (0-6); 8-14 (1-10); 1-7 (4-11).
Field size: 16+ (5-19); 15- (0-8).

Note: The above stats are based on runs for Milton Bradley (he's one of a handful with whom previous trainer, Sir Mark Prescott, never quite got to grips).

Combine 5f with good or faster ground, a big field (16+) and an absence of less than seven days and his record becomes: 11101 (4-5), the only defeat coming when impossibly drawn at Beverley. It was some effort to win from stall 1 of 19 at Chepstow last September, and it would come as no surprise to see him take that next step this year.

INDIAN SPARK

Distance: 5f (7-33); 6f (4-40); 7f+ (0-3).
Going: Firm (1-5); G-F (2-22); Good (3-21); G-S (2-12); Soft (2-11); Heavy (1-5).
Field size: 20+ (1-22); 16-19 (2-16); 15- (8-38).

Although he has won in fields of 18, 19 and 20, in each case the runners split into at least two groups, and he effectively raced within fields of 8, 11 and 6 (from a starting position of 1, 4 and 6 stalls off a favoured rail respectively). Combine 5f with fields of 15 or fewer and his record becomes: 1024155941132 (4-13), his last three runs seeing him, from left to right, finish: 1st – in a Listed race at Chester, 3rd – beaten 0.5l in a hot conditions race, and 2nd – beaten a head in a Group 3. With a handicap mark of 106, Listed races now look the best option, particularly as he's more likely to get the small field he needs in that company, and he certainly showed plenty on his comeback at Doncaster. Impossibly drawn, he did best of his group, running on well late on ground softer than ideal.

JAWHARI

Distance: 5f (5-15); 6f (0-12); 7f+ (1-6).
Going: G-F (2-8); Good (1-8); G-S (0-4); Soft (0-2); Heavy (0-1); AWT (3-10).
Fresh (first two runs of the season, first two runs after a long break (four months+) or after break of six weeks+): (6-18).

Combine 5f with good or faster ground or an All-Weather surface, and running fresh (his record fresh for Terry Mills being: 132115 (3-6)) and his record becomes: 10711211 (5-8). From left to right: 1st, 0 – poorly drawn in stall 4 at Goodwood (first three drawn 17, 13 and 14 of 17), 7th – All-Weather debut and poorly drawn on the inside at Wolverhampton, 1st, 1st, 2nd – beaten in a photo, 1st and 1st. He is one to watch first time on Turf, and when running fresh after that, particularly having shown himself as good as ever with an easy Wolverhampton win on 11 February.

JUWWI

Distance: 5f (7-35); 6f (7-82); 7f+ (0-10).
Going: Firm (2-5); G-F (3-21); Good (2-29); G-S (1-12); Soft (0-16); Heavy (0-7); Equitrack (0-4); Fibresand (Slow) (1-6); Fibresand (Standard) (5-27).
Fresh (absence since last run): 28 days+ (1-11); 20-27 (0-7); 13-19 (2-20); 6-12 (6-60); 5 (0-4); 4 (0-8); 3 (1-5); 2 (1-5); 1 (3-7).
Course: flat (12-88); undulating (2-39).
Field size: 15+ (8-68); 14- (6-59).

Combine sprints distances with good or faster ground (or Fibresand), a flat track, a break of 19 days or fewer since his last run and a big field (15 or more) and his record becomes: 8101551612180009 (5-16). Under these conditions but having his second runs in two days, this improves to: 119 (2-3). He starts the season fairly rated, having peaked at 90 last July, particularly given that he improved his All-Weather mark by a stone over the winter. His two runs in successive days at Doncaster's Lincoln meeting were good, on ground softer than ideal (second of far-side group when sixth overall and then never near the favoured stands' rail when fourth overall).

LATE NIGHT OUT

Distance: 6f (1-5); 7f (6-20); 1m (1-7).
Going: G-F+ (1-7); Good (3-9); G-S- (4-15); AWT (0-1).
Fresh (first two runs of the year, or after break of six weeks+ (UK)): (5-11).
Course (UK only): straight (2-10); round (6-15).
Overseas form: (0-7).

He hasn't won on a straight course since October '98; combine 7f with good or softer ground on UK round courses and his record becomes: 314451111 (5-9). Knocking out runs when not fresh, this improves to: 3111 (3-4).

Juwwi is happiest in a big field on a flat course, and after a recent outing

LION'S DOMANE

Distance: 5f (0-1); 6f (0-3); 7f (5-16); 1m+ (0-7).
Going: Firm (0-1); G-F (4-9); Good (1-7); G-S (0-2); Soft (0-1); AWT (0-7).
Course: straight (0-8); round (5-19).

Combine 7f with good to firm or faster ground on round courses and his record becomes: 11110 (4-5), with his sole defeat at York forgivable on account of being unable to dominate a field of 23. He looks one to follow this season, especially at Chester, Musselburgh or Thirsk (he has yet to win elsewhere).

LOVE'S DESIGN (IRE)

Distance: 6f (0-6); 7f (2-12); 1m (5-13); 1m1f+ (0-2).
Going: G-F+ (0-9); Good (2-6); G-S- (0-4); Equi (4-4); Poly (1-4); Fibre (0-6).
Course: straight (0-10); round (7-22).
Class: C+ (0-7); D- (7-25).

Looking solely at his 7f-1m runs on a fast surface (excluding good to soft or softer turf and Fibresand), in Class D or lower company, his record becomes: 11111441710 (7-11). He looked as good as ever when winning on the Polytrack in December and starts the Turf season reasonably handicapped on 73.

MAMMAS F-C (IRE)

Distance: 5f (5-24); 6f (4-25); 7f (1-3).
Going: Firm+ (2-5); G-F (6-19); Good (1-8); G-S- (0-5); AWT (1-15).
Fresh (break): 22 days+ (0-8); 15-21 (3-12); 8-14 (4-20); 1-7 (3-12).

Combine 5f with good to firm or faster ground and racing within 21 days
of her last run and her record becomes: 61153114 (4-8). From left to right:
6th – for her previous trainer, 1st, 1st, 5th – poorly drawn when an outlier
at Beverley (first seven drawn 14, 16, 8, 9, 1, 12 and 15 of 15), 3rd – an
outlier at Warwick (first four drawn 5, 4, 10 and 1 of 11), 1st, 1st, and 4th
– drawn widest of all when a 20-day absence would have been on the long
side. Since returning from an injury sustained in a fall at Windsor in
March 2000, she's looked better suited by 5f; although she did win at 6f
last year, it came in a small field (nine), and she would only be of interest
at the longer trip if encountering similar conditions this term.

MARSAD (IRE)

Distance: 5f (0-4); 6f (3-34); 7f (0-3).
Going: G-F (0-12); Good (1-12); G-S (1-6); Soft (1-7); Heavy (0-4).
Fresh (first three runs of the season or after break of six weeks+): (3-20).

Combine 6f with good or softer ground and running fresh, and his record
becomes: 1331550291 (3-10). From left to right: 1st, 3rd – beaten two necks
in a field of 29 at Newmarket, 3rd – beaten two heads in a 13-runner
Kempton handicap, 1st, 5th – first home on the stands' side in the Great
St Wilfrid at Ripon (first five drawn 17, 21, 22, 18 and 4 of 23), 5th – poorly
drawn in an 18-runner Kempton handicap, finishing second in his group,
0 – 13th of 28 in Newmarket handicap, racing up the unfavoured stands'
side (finishing second in his group), 2nd – of 21 at Goodwood, 9th – of 22
in a Doncaster handicap (missed the break and hampered), and 1st. While
his strike-rate under ideal conditions is not great, he's almost invariably
run in big-field, competitive handicaps and hasn't always been favoured by
the draw. Watch him when his mark drops back into the 80s.

MOUSEHOLE

Distance: 5f (11-75); 6f (1-17).
Going: Firm (3-6); G-F (8-40); Good (1-32); G-S (0-6); Soft (0-6); Hvy (0-2).
Month: Apr-May (1-23); Jun (3-21); Jul (5-14); Aug (3-15); Sept-Oct (0-19).

Combine 5f with good to firm or faster ground and racing between June
and August, and his record becomes: 2130103212017421112811881887124824
(9-30). In Class E grade or below, this improves to: 1103121721112824 (7-
16). Basically, he can't have the going too fast, and Rae Guest took him to
Nottingham last June purely because the watering system had broken
down and the ground was hard.

MY BROTHER

Distance: 5f (0-2); 6f (1-4); 7f (0-7); 1m+ (0-3).
Going: G-F+ (0-10); Good (1-5); AWT (0-1).
Fresh (seasonal debut): (1-5).

Lightly-raced for an eight-year-old, with just 16 starts to his name, his two comeback runs since joining his current trainer have produced a win at 33-1, and a second at 16-1 (both over 6f at Goodwood). Although never one to take a short price about, he's worth keeping an eye on if reappearing at the Sussex track this season (the style of racing there suits him).

NIGRASINE

Distance: 5f (0-2); 6f (7-39); 7f (1-16); 1m+ (1-16).
Going: G-F+ (5-20); Good (4-30); G-S (0-11); Soft / Heavy (0-7); AWT (0-5).
Field size: 20+ (0-28); 14-19 (1-11); 10-13 (2-13); 9- (6-21).
Class: A (1-15); B (0-29); C (5-16); D (3-10); E- (0-3).

Combine good or faster ground with racing in Class C or lower company and his record becomes: 1141111076201950915 (8-19). Looking only at runs in fields of 13 or fewer, this improves to: 1141111215 (7-10); knock out runs at any trip other than 6f and his record is better still: 11411111 (7-8), the only defeat coming as a juvenile back in September '96. Although he's won a Class A, that came in June '98, when allowed an easy lead in a seven-runner Listed Haydock event. He did best of the stands-side group at Ripon on 2 April and looks as good as ever.

NORTHERN SVENGALI (IRE)

Distance: 5f (4-43); 6f (1-21); 7f (0-5).
Going: Firm (1-7); G-F (3-21); Good / G-S (1-24); Soft– (0-4); AWT (0-13).
Class: C+ (0-9); D (1-24); E (3-20); F (1-16).

Combine 5f with good to firm or faster ground in Class E or lower company, and his record becomes: 203181015809 (3-12). When returned to the track within four days, this improves to: 311019 (3-6). Basically, cross him off if he's not racing over 5f at Class E level or below (his only 6f win, and his only Class D win, came in a weak Catterick juvenile maiden).

NOW LOOK HERE

Distance: 5f (0-6); 6f (1-19); 7f (1-10).
Going: G-F+ (0-11); Good (0-7); G-S (0-7); Soft / Heavy (2-10).
Fresh (after break of six weeks+): (2-8).
Class: Group 1-3 (0-5); Listed (1-8); B- (1-22).

Combine 6f-7f with good to soft or softer ground, at Listed class or lower, when fresh, and his record becomes: 611 (2-3), the only defeat coming when running green on his racecourse debut at two.

Now Look Here is always worth watching fresh and when the ground is soft

PANDJOJOE (IRE)

Distance: 5f (0-8); 6f (4-24); 7f+ (0-4).
Going: G-F+ (1-10); Good (2-10); G-S (0-3); Soft (1-4); Hvy (0-4); AWT (0-5).
Fresh: first three runs of the season (4-12); fourth run or later (0-24).

Looking solely at his runs at 6f on his first, second or third start of the season, his record becomes: 11151 (4-5), the only defeat coming when an outlier at Thirsk (first seven home drawn 15, 17, 20, 21, 2, 22 and 24 of 23). He starts this year well handicapped on 59, having won at Hamilton last July off 61.

PATRICIAN FOX (IRE)

Distance: 5f (2-16); 6f (0-7).
Going: G-F (1-4); Good (0-7); G-S (0-3); Soft (1-3); Hvy (0-3); AWT (0-3).
Fresh (after break of five weeks+): (2-4).

Look solely at her runs over 5f when fresh, and her record becomes: 711 (2-3), the seventh coming on her racecourse debut at two (when she missed the break and ran green). Beverley seems to suit, and she starts the year well weighted on 55, having won there (on ground slightly faster than ideal) off 62 last June.

PATSY CULSYTH

Distance: 5f (1-16); 6f (2-17); 7f+ (1-14).
Going: G-F+ (0-16); Good (3-11); G-S (1-7); Soft (0-6); Hvy (0-3); AWT (0-4).
Course: Newcastle (2-6); others (2-41).
Race type: handicaps (0-22); claimers (1-7); sellers (3-11); others (0-7).

Although her seasonal debut record is only: 62910 (1-5), she's had valid excuses for the defeats; from left to right: 6th – racecourse debut over an inadequate 5f, 2nd – an outlier at Thirsk (first three drawn 20, 6 and 22 of 23), 9th – All-Weather, 1st – won at 33-1, and 0 – All-Weather (in four starts on the sand she's been beaten 13l, 46l, 8l and 11l+). While no world-beater, she'll be of interest if reappearing at Newcastle; her course record in sellers being: 211 (2-3), the only defeat coming by a short-head.

PAYS D'AMOUR (IRE)

Distance: 5f (0-1); 6f (2-15); 7f (1-12); 1m (0-1).
Going: G-F+ (2-10); Good (1-9); G-S (0-5); Soft (0-4); AWT (0-1).
Fresh (seasonal debut): (0-4).
Race value: £10,000+ (0-8); £9,999- (3-21).

Combine 6f-7f with good or faster ground with a race value of less than £10,000, and starting for the second time or later within a season, and his record becomes: 51212139243 (3-11). Although twice a winner round Epsom, there's a case for him being better suited by stiff courses, his Newmarket record being a short-head second in a huge field, an outlying third behind Lord Pacal (first six drawn 29, 28, 3, 20, 23 and 22 of 29) and a third at 50-1 in the Bunbury Cup last year.

PETARGA

Distance: 5f (2-9); 6f (3-26).
Going: Firm (0-2); G-F (2-18); Good (2-13); G-S (1-1); Soft (0-1).
Fresh (break): 21 days+ (0-15); 15-20 (3-6); 8-14 (2-11); 7- (0-3).
Field size: 12+ (4-25); 11- (1-10).
Class: C+ (0-12); D- (5-23).

Combine running in Class D company or below with an absence of 20 days or shorter and her record becomes: 21470210110410 (5-14). At 6f only this improves to: 2021011 (3-7), the two unplaced efforts coming after inadequate breaks of three and seven days. Although she has a better strike-rate at 5f, James Toller believes she's better at longer trips, and this is backed up by her only 5f win since her juvenile season coming at stiff Leicester on dead ground.

PICCOLO CATIVO

Distance: 5f (3-16); 6f (3-20); 7f (1-11); 1m (0-6).
Going: G-F+ (0-11); Good (1-9); G-S (2-7); Soft (2-13); Heavy (1-3); AWT (1-10).
Fresh (first two runs of the season or after break of six weeks+): (5-14).

Despite a decent strike-rate at 5f, she is no longer suited by the minimum (two of her three wins at it coming at two, the other early on at three) and she has lost her last ten 5f starts, a run stretching back to June '98. Combine a distance of 6f-7f (and 5f pre-July '98) with good to soft or softer ground and her record becomes: 61240418192211 (5-14). Add in the proviso that she must be fresh and this improves to: 01191 (3-5), the wins coming at 33-1, 12-1 and 6-1. She may need to come down a few pounds from 55 but will be worth watching when the ground eases at the end of August / early September.

PLEASURE TIME

Going: Firm (2-5); G-F (4-26); Good (1-19); G-S- (0-10); AWT (1-4).
Course: flat (7-38); undulating (1-26).
Fresh (absence since last run): 29 days+ (4-16); 15-28 (4-23); 14- (0-25).

Combine a flat track and good to firm or faster ground (or All-Weather track) with a break of 15 days or more and his record becomes: 115001120361231 (6-15), with him either winning or being an outlier on his last four such starts. Concentrate only on runs after a break of six weeks or more, and his figures improve to: 11231 (3-5); from left to right: 1st, 1st, 2nd – beaten 0.75l by Mousehole (who was facing his ideal conditions), 3rd – an outlier at Southwell (racing away from the main field) and 1st.

POP THE CORK

Distance: 5f (4-22); 6f (0-1).
Going: Firm (1-2); G-F (3-10); Good (0-6); G-S (0-2); AWT (0-3).
Fresh (first two runs of the season or after break of six weeks+): (0-7).

Combine 5f with good to firm or firmer ground, and knock out runs when fresh, and his record becomes: 1803167113 (4-10). At Musselburgh only, this improves to: 111 (3-3); this is a course that clearly suits, with him winning there on consecutive days last August (he's also won twice by racing towards the far side from a high draw). Although he starts this season on a rating of 69, which is 6lb above his highest winning mark, his last two runs of '01, on ground softer than ideal, suggest he is capable of scoring off it. The chances are he'll show signs of coming to hand before winning in any case.

PRINCESS ALMORA

Distance: 6f (3-8); 7f (0-3).
Going: G-F (2-7); Good (1-3); G-S (0-1).
Course: flat (3-6); undulating (0-5)
Position from favoured rail: (6f only): 3 stalls or less (3-3); 4 stalls+ (0-5).

Although twice a runner-up when tried over 7f (beaten only 0.5l and a neck), both times she was found slowly-run, small-field races, and she's much happier at six. Granted that trip on a flat track and from a draw near the rail, she should win races this year, and watch for her at Windsor, where her record reads: 121 (2-3).

PRIX STAR

Distance: 5f (1-7); 6f (4-40); 7f (0-13).
Going: G-F+ (1-24); Good (3-14); G-S (1-7); Soft (0-7); Hvy (0-2); AWT (0-6).

Combine 6f with a draw of within three stalls of a rail and his record over the past two seasons becomes: 924120110 (3-9). From left to right: 9th – third on the far side at Nottingham, 2nd – despite looking in need of his seasonal debut, 4th – second on the wrong side at Kempton, 1st, 2nd – won the far-side race at Hamilton, 0 – third on the wrong side at York, 1st, 1st, and 0 – no chance racing alone up the unfavoured rail at Redcar. Looking only at his runs over 6f when drawn within three stalls of a favoured rail, his record is: 2111 (3-4). He starts this season on a rating of 69, just 1lb higher than when successful at Newmarket.

PTARMIGAN RIDGE

Distance: 5f (4-20); 6f+ (0-5).
Going: G-F (0-1); Good (1-7); G-S (0-4); Soft (3-8); Heavy (0-5).
Fresh (absence since last run): 42 days+ (2-4); 21-41 (1-7); 20- (1-14).

Combine 5f with an absence of six weeks or more and his record becomes: 115 (2-3), the defeat coming when poorly drawn in 12 at York (first five drawn 3, 1, 2, 4 and 12 of 15). Unbeaten in two starts around a turn (both at Catterick), he would be of interest if sent to Chester this year, although he may need to come down a few pounds from 84.

REDOUBTABLE (USA)

Distance: 5f (2-6); 6f (6-47); 7f (7-55); 1m (0-12).
Going: Firm (1-5); G-F (3-30); Good (1-19); G-S (1-10); Soft– (2-12); AWT (7-44).

Since the start of 2000, he has performed poorly in handicaps (1-34), but in Classified Stakes, he's been more impressive: 1041433111220000 (5-16). Combine 6f-7f with running in a Classified Stakes and his record becomes: 104143311100 (5-12); when starting at 10-1 or shorter this improves to: 11433111 (5-8). He starts this season well handicapped on Turf on 58.

REGAL SONG (IRE)

Distance: 5f (5-26); 6f (0-14); 7f (0-3).
Going: G-F (0-4); Good (1-7); G-S (0-5); Soft (2-11); Heavy (2-7); AWT (0-9).
Headgear: blinkers (4-29), none (1-14).
Position from the favoured rail: (ie, 1 = drawn next to rail): 1 (1-3); 2 (2-3); 3 (0-0); 4 (0-1); 5 (2-3); 6+ (0-33).

Combine 5f with good to soft or softer ground and a draw within five stalls of the favoured rail, and his record becomes: 311101 (4-6). While he's worn blinkers for five of his six wins, he won on his only start without them, but soft ground is a must (his only win on good came when 6-4 favourite for an eight-runner Hamilton maiden). Tim Etherington has always thought a lot of him and he'll be placed to advantage once more when dropping to a rating of below 80.

RITA'S ROCK APE

Distance: 5f (8-55); 6f (0-1).
Going: Firm (3-7); G-F (4-23); Good (1-15); G-S (0-3); Soft (0-1); AWT (0-7).

A front-runner who shows a marked tendency to drift right in the closing stages of her races (a trait that has cost her victory more than once), she'll win again this year when handed a draw next to a right-hand rail on fast ground. She only came across those conditions once last season – when making all to win at 9-1 at Salisbury in June – and finds herself back on the same mark again thanks to six subsequent defeats. Craig Carver seems to get on particularly well with her.

ROSES OF SPRING

Distance: 5f (0-3); 6f (1-10); 7f (0-2).
Going: Firm (0-4); G-F (1-4); Good (0-2); G-S (0-3); AWT (0-2).

She ran well from a poor draw more than once last season, most notably at Thirsk in August, when second on firm ground over 6f (first six drawn 16, 2, 15, 19, 17 and 20 of 20). Although still to win at 5f (she's been beaten a short-head and failed to take to a first-time visor in two attempts) time may show it to be her optimum distance and she could well run up a sequence this season in small fields on fast ground.

RUSHCUTTER BAY

Distance: 5f (4-31); 6f (3-23).
Going: G-F+ (3-28); Good (4-18); G-S (0-4); Soft– (0-3); AWT: (0-1).
Fresh (first two runs of the season or after break of six weeks+): (3-18).
Course: Newmarket (4-15); others (2-39).

Looking solely at his runs over 5f (his three 6f wins came in fields of 12, 8 and 10 and he doesn't get that trip at the level he now contests) at Newmarket, his record becomes: 2211 (2-4). Don't rule out a repeat victory in the Palace House granted decent ground, and hopefully that will be his comeback.

Rushcutter Bay (No. 10) has an exceptional record over 5f at Newmarket

RYEFIELD

Distance: 6f (2-17); 7f (2-17); 1m (2-21).
Going: Firm (1-6); G-F (4-15); Good (0-16); G-S (0-7); Soft (0-7); Heavy (1-4).
Course: Ayr (4-19); others (2-36).
Ayr by distance: 6f (2-7); 7f (1-6); 1m (1-6).
'Fresh Ayr' (absence since last run): 6 days+ (1-16); 1-5 (3-3).

He clearly goes well off the back of a very recent run, and should be followed closely when turned out quickly over 6f at Ayr this season (his best efforts over 7f and a mile have come on fast ground and in small fields, when the emphasis hasn't been on stamina). He's been beaten on his last 24 starts away from Ayr.

SAND HAWK

Distance: 5f (0-1); 6f (0-15); 7f (6-29); 1m+ (0-13).
Going: Firm (0-2); G-F (0-7); Good (0-4); G-S (1-8); Soft– (0-7); AWT (5-0).
Fresh (absence since last run): 8 days+ (1-41); 7- (5-17).

Combine 7f with good to soft or softer ground (or Fibresand) when running within seven days of his previous start, and his record becomes: 211122101 (5-9). From left to right: 2nd – beaten a neck, 1st, 1st, 1st, 2nd – beaten 0.5l when winning the far-side race at Chepstow, 2nd – beaten a neck, 1st, 0 – outclassed in a £10,000 Class C event, and 1st. He starts the year on a handy mark.

Seven No Trumps (left) seems to reach his peak in May

SEVEN NO TRUMPS

Distance: 5f (2-7); 6f (4-24); 7f (0-1).
Going: Firm (1-1); G-F (2-10); Good (1-7); G-S (0-8); Soft (1-5); Heavy (1-1).
Fresh (seasonal debut): (1-4).
Class: A (0-6); B (2-11); C (1-9); D- (3-6).
Month: Mar-Apr (1-3); May (4-6); June-Aug (0-13); Sept (0-6); Oct (1-4).

Combine 5f-6f with racing at Class B or lower on his second start of the season or later, and knock out June-August, and his record becomes: 110200112031 (5-12). Look solely at May and this improves to: 1111 (4-4). He was impressive at on his Doncaster comeback given that Barry Hills thought him short of 100% and further improvement can be expected.

SHARP HAT

Distance: 5f (9-50); 6f (4-45); 7f+ (0-5).
Fresh (absence since last run): 42 days+ (0-9); 41- (13-91).
Field size: 20+ (1-23); 16-19 (2-22); 12-15 (1-26); 11- (9-28).

The more recent his previous run the better he seems to perform, and the last three times he's returned to the track within three days he's finished: 121 (2-3), the second coming when beaten a neck in last year's Ayr Silver Cup. Combine 5f with a small field (11 or less) and a return to action within six weeks, and his record becomes: 7713616111118 (7-13). From left to right: 7th – no obvious excuse, 7th – badly hampered at Chester, 1st, 3rd

– at Wolverhampton from a difficult draw, 6th – beaten by his draw at
Hamilton despite the small field, 1st, 6th – beaten by the draw at
Newcastle, 1st, 1st, 1st, 1st, 1st, 8th and 8th. As effective over 6f when
handed fast ground and a small field, he won all three of his turf starts in
small fields last season.

Sharp Hat has an excellent record when turned out again quickly

SILKEN WINGS (IRE)

Distance: 5f (0-3); 6f (1-10); 6f110y+ (0-4).
Going: Firm (0-2); G-F (1-2); Good (0-4); Soft (0-1); AWT (0-8).

In four turf runs at 6f she has finished out of the frame just once, and given
that trip, fast ground and a rail to run against, she'll win again this season.
Formerly with Ian Balding, she showed she retained her ability when finishing second after a break on her first All-Weather start for Reg
Hollinshead in December.

SIR DESMOND

Distance: 5f (2-12); 6f (0-5).
Going: Firm (1-3); G-F (0-5); Good (1-4); G-S (0-4); Heavy (0-1).
Course: flat (2-9); undulating (0-8).

Combine 5f with a flat track and his record becomes: 311272 (2-6). From
left to right: 3rd – in a Doncaster maiden on his first attempt at 5f, 1st, 1st,
2nd – beaten 0.5l in an 18-runner event at Kempton, 7th – in a hot York
handicap, and 2nd – poorly drawn at Windsor. Also desperately drawn

when third at Beverley (1 of 17) and at Leicester (first four drawn 19, 18, 9 and 17 of 21) last season off 75, he starts this season on 78 and will only need luck with the draw to win a few.

Smart Predator (in front) is still relatively unexposed at the minimum trip

SMART PREDATOR

Distance: 5f (5-13); 6f (0-13); 7f (2-14).
Going: G-F+ (4-16); Good (1-11); G-S (2-5); Soft (0-6); Heavy (0-2).

Combine 5f with good to soft or faster ground and his record becomes: 0121910211 (5-10). From left to right: 0 – no chance from stall 1 at Beverley, 1st, 2nd – an outlier at Yarmouth (first four drawn 18, 2, 19 and 14 of 18), 1st, 9th – from a moderate draw (11) at Musselburgh in a race where low numbers were favoured, 1st, 0 – no obvious excuse, although he faded as if having a problem, 2nd – stall opened late in the Epsom race that should have been declared void, and 1st – at Beverley despite a moderate draw. Both his 7f wins came when making all in small fields; expect him to prove Group class over 5f this year.

SOAKED

Distance: 5f (11-65); 6f (3-16); 7f+ (0-10).
Going: Firm (0-3); G-F (3-21); Good (3-18); G-S (2-10); Soft / Heavy (0-6); AWT Equitrack (3-7); Fibresand (3-26).
Fresh (absence since last run): 17 days+ (1-30); 16 or fewer (13-61).

Since March '98, when he recorded his first win after almost two years' racing, his record over 5f when returned to the track within 16 days is: 341211110146133648211402039212147700203 (11-39). Concentrating only on Turf runs between May and August and at below Class C, this improves to: 121421140209211770 (6-18). A 5f specialist (his sole win at 6f coming in a Southwell seller), he starts the year handily weighted on 67, 2lb lower than the mark off which he ran so well into second at Leicester last September.

SOBA JONES

Distance: 5f (2-17); 6f (1-5); 7f+ (0-4).
Going: Firm (0-2); G-F (1-8); Good (2-8); G-S (0-2); Soft (0-4); AWT (0-2).
Field size: 11+ (0-20); 10- (3-6).

Combine 5f-6f with a small field (ten runners or fewer) on Turf and his record becomes: 3111 (3-4), the only defeat coming on his racecourse debut as a two-year-old. His seven runs in the summer of last year (June-August) stand up to close scrutiny: 1802501 (2-7). From left to right: 1st, 8th – drawn down the wrong side at Ripon, 0 – didn't seem to handle Hamilton (drawn wrong anyway), 2nd – raced wide apart from Flak Jacket on unsuitably soft ground at Haydock, 5th – impossibly drawn in 8 of 17 at Beverley (only beaten 2+l), 0 – impossibly drawn in 5 of 20 at Beverley (raced stands' side) and 1st. He starts the season rated 70, just 1lb higher than for his last win at Catterick.

SPENCERS WOOD (IRE)

Distance: 6f (3-4); 7f (1-6); 1m+ (0-4).
Going: G-F (1-5); Good (1-6); G-S (1-1); Soft (1-2).
Fresh (after break of six weeks+): (2-5).

Combine 6f with good to soft or softer ground and his record becomes: 110 (2-3), the only defeat coming in Italy at the tail end of last season (probably over the top). Now Peter Makin knows soft ground is probably what he needs (his only win on good to firm came when outclassing a moderate bunch at Hamilton), don't be surprised to see him campaigned successfully at Group level abroad.

SUPERFRILLS

Distance: 5f (3-54); 6f (3-25).
Going: Good+ (0-33); G-S (1-10); Soft (2-9); Heavy (0-3); Fibresand (3-24).

Combine 6f with good to soft or softer turf, or Fibresand, and her record becomes: 28927402342818700010130 (3-23). Knock out all runs when she hasn't been drawn within two stalls of the inside rail on a left-handed track, or within two stalls from either rail on a straight course, and her record improves to: 24211 (2-5), the wins coming at 50-1 and 25-1.

TALBOT AVENUE

Distance: 5f (1-6); 6f (0-6).
Going: G-F (1-7); Good (0-4); Soft (0-1).
Fresh (after break of six weeks+): (0-4).

Combine 5f with any ground and exclude runs when fresh, and his record becomes: 54162 (1-5). From left to right: 5th – only beaten 2l from a middle draw at Chester, 4th – did best of the top half in the draw at Chester, 1st, 6th – only beaten 2l by the progressive Jessica's Dream, and 2nd – (of 18) at Goodwood.

TARAS EMPEROR (IRE)

Distance: 5f (4-13); 6f (0-6); 7f+ (0-3).
Going: G-F (0-7); Good (0-3); G-S (0-4); Soft (1-5); Heavy (3-3).

Combine 5f with soft or heavy ground and his record becomes: 411117 (4-6). Put simply, the softer the ground the better he performs, and he may also be capable of winning at 6f given suitable underfoot conditions. Well backed on his return he'll win again this year.

TAYIF

Distance: 5f (1-3); 6f (2-7); 7f (2-12).
Going: G-F+ (1-4); Good (3-9); G-S (1-6); Soft (0-3).

Both his 7f wins came in slowly-run races for Pip Payne and 6f seems his optimum, as demonstrated by his Ayr Silver Cup win last season. Since joining David Nicholls, he has won two of his six starts at 6f, both on flat tracks (York and Ayr) and in big fields (23 and 27 runners). His two defeats under ideal conditions came on his comeback at Doncaster, when poorly drawn, and at York in a race where the prominent-racers were favoured. Don't be surprised to see him progress further (his rumoured breathing problems now look behind him) and the Stewards' Cup and Ayr Gold Cup would seem ideal targets.

TECHNICIAN (IRE)

Distance: 5f (0-3); 6f (4-27); 7f (1-34); 1m+ (0-11).
Going: Firm (2-6); G-F (1-15); Good (1-16); G-S- (0-20); AWT (1-18).
Going (6f only, fast ground): Firm (2-3); G-F (1-8); Good (1-5).
Fresh (absence since last run): 29 days+ (0-11); 28- (5-64).

Combine 6f with good or faster ground and a return to action within 28 days, and his record becomes: 3021232220121421 (4-16).

THAT MAN AGAIN

Distance: 5f (13-87); 6f (0-11).
Going (5f only): Firm (2-6); G-F (8-36); Good (2-22); G-S (1-11); Soft / Heavy (0-4); AWT (0-8).
Field size (5f only): 16+ (1-21); 12-15 (4-35); 11- (8-31).

Combine 5f with good or faster going (Turf) and a small field (11 or fewer), and his record becomes: 124143442141146145310 (7-21). Always done best racing next to a right-hand rail, and ideally needs to be drawn next to the fence, or only have hold-up horses outside. Look for him at Sandown and Salisbury.

THE TRADER

Distance: 5f (5-17); 6f (0-5); 7f (0-1).
Going: G-F+ (5-10); Good (0-4); G-S (0-4); Soft (0-5).
Headgear: blinkers (3-8); none (2-15).

Combine 5f with good to firm or firmer ground and his record becomes: 21141115 (5-8). Knock out those runs when he hasn't worn blinkers, and this improves to: 1115 (3-4), his only defeat coming at a price of 56-1, when beaten just over 1l in the Grade 2 Hong Kong Sprint at Sha Tin last December.

TIME N TIME AGAIN

Distance: 5f (2-11); 6f (0-1).
Going: Good+ (2-8); G-S- (0-4).
Fresh (seasonal debut): (2-2).

Having won first time out as a two-year-old (20-1), he repeated the dose last season at 10-1, and may be capable of winning mid-season when returning from a rest. Although he's lost all four such starts to date, he's faced some impossible tasks, including at Royal Ascot, and he will be worth backing on his comeback if handed 5f, fast ground and a decent draw, perhaps back at Chester.

Vision Of Night (far side) has won 8 from 10 when tackling a small field on fast ground

VISION OF NIGHT

Distance: 5f (0-2); 6f (8-17); 6f110y+ (0-2).
Going: Good+ (8-17); G-S- (0-4).
Field size: 11+ (1-9); 10- (7-12).

Combine a small field (ten or fewer) with fast ground (good or firmer) and a trip of 6f and his record becomes: 2113111111 (8-10). From left to right: 2nd – beaten a neck on his racecourse debut, 1st, 1st, 3rd – on ground slower than the official good judging by the time taken being 3secs slower than standard, 1st, 1st, 1st, 1st, 1st and 1st.

VITA SPERICOLATA (IRE)

Distance: 5f (3-22); 6f (1-7); 7f (0-1).
Going: G-F+ (2-11); Good (2-11); G-S (0-3); Soft / Heavy (0-5).
Field size: 12+ (0-11); 11- (4-19).
Class: A (2-20); B (0-4); C (1-5); D- (1-1); the problem with breaking down class in this way is that it doesn't differentiate between a £10,000 Listed race and a £100,000 Group race (both Class A), and race value provides a clearer picture of her class barrier:
Value (to winner): £15,000+ (0-18); £14,999- (4-10).

Combine a small field (11 or fewer) with good or faster ground in races worth less than £15,000 and her record becomes: 1213311 (4-7). From left to right: 1st, 2nd – the going was softer than the official good (with the final time being 3secs slower than standard), 1st, 3rd – didn't get home over 6f at two, 3rd – beaten in a three-way photo, 1st and 1st.

WHO GOES THERE

Distance: 6f (0-3); 7f (3-22); 1m+ (0-20).
Going: Firm (1-4); G-F (2-19); Good (0-10); G-S (0-3); Soft (0-4); AWT (0-5).
Course: straight (3-18); round (0-27).

Combine a straight 7f with good or faster ground and her record becomes: 202117705515 (3-12). From left to right: 2nd – in a Folkestone claimer at 50-1, 0 – poorly drawn at Yarmouth in stall 13 (five of first six drawn in single figures), 2nd – an outlier at Chepstow (beaten by a neck at 33-1), 1st, 1st, 7th – very slowly away at Folkestone, 7th – slowly away and poorly drawn at Folkestone, 0 – poorly drawn at Lingfield, 5th – an outlier at Chepstow (first six drawn 16, 13, 17, 12, 7 and 15 of 20), 5th – slowly away at Chepstow (but only beaten 11+ in a field of 19), 1st, 5th – up in class at Newmarket (but only beaten 3l), and 5th – poorly drawn at Chepstow. While her propensity to start slowly will always make things difficult, she's again going to be worth following on straight tracks, and is worth noting if sent for the Lingfield fillies' handicap she's won the past two Augusts.

Vita Spericolata (right) has a definite class barrier

ZUHAIR

Distance: 5f (4-27); 6f (5-53); 7f+ (0-3).

Going: Firm (0-2); G-F (6-23); Good (2-33); G-S- (0-19); AWT (1-6).

Combine 5f-6f with good to firm or faster ground and his record becomes: 3153002621411001974553219 (6-25). For David Nicholls only, this improves to 5-18. The winner of the Charlton Handicap, over 5f at Glorious Goodwood, for the past three seasons, his record at Goodwood bears close inspection: 511015514319 (5-12). Looking only at runs on good to firm or faster going, this improves to: 111431 (4-6). Concentrate only on runs at 5f and we're left with: 111 (3-3). There's no point putting him up as one to follow at Goodwood, as his chance there is usually covered in the prices; instead watch him when he goes to York or Lingfield (Turf). The latter course, like Goodwood, has a significant downhill section, as does Epsom, where he ran well from a poor draw last year. He ran alright on his Ripon comeback.

CHAPTER 4

Outliers

Graham Wheldon

The subject of what an outlier is, and how to pinpoint them, has already been covered in depth in my two previous books on the draw, so I won't go into too much detail (largely because space doesn't allow). In a nutshell, though, an outlier is a horse who has run well from a poor draw.

To keep track of outliers, you can either apply the draw biases listed in the first section of this book to every race run, or pick up a copy of the *Racing & Football Outlook* and find them neatly laid out for you. Nothing quite like free advertising!

I've always advised only backing outliers on their next outing if they meet the following six requirements:

The ground is suitable – the selection must have won, or at least shown very good form, on the prevailing going.

The trip is suitable – the selection is not stepping up to 7f for the first time having caught the eye over a sprint trip, unless he seems likely to be suited by it.

The Handicapper has not raised the rating a ridiculous amount – the selection is not asked to race off a much higher mark than when it was noted. Anything more than a 3lb rise is pushing the limits.

The race is similar in class to the time before – the selection has not gone up from, for example, a Class F handicap, to a Class C handicap.

The selection has not been off the course for any length of time – any longer than a six-week absence may suggest some sort of problem.

Most importantly, the selection has a reasonable draw – if the draw is again against him, he may run above expectations once more, but is likely to be facing another impossible task.

When to scratch outliers

If an outlier goes on to win next time, he should then almost always come off the list as he's done what had been hoped for, but what to do if he does not have everything in his favour next time is down to the individual.

For example, if a horse does not have the ground in his favour for his next run, or he has gone up 4lb or more in the weights, he will become a no-bet, and a decision has to be made after he's run as to whether or not to keep him on the list.

If he's run well, the advice nine times out of ten is to retain him; if he runs poorly, cross him out but don't forget about him completely, and still keep an eye out for him when he is next facing the conditions under which he originally caught the eye.

AMERICAN COUSIN

A regular winner over the past three seasons, he's as reliable as clockwork and starts the year on a mark of 66, 2lb below his last winning rating, at York last July, and 4lb below the figure off which he started his handicap career with Brian Meehan at two. Always worth watching at Beverley (he's won his next start on three separate occasions after running well there from a poor draw), don't think about backing him until June (by which time David Nicholls will have got him a few pounds lower still) and until after he's shown signs of a comeback.

BARITONE

He hardly ever races on Turf – he's rated a stone and a half better on the All-Weather – but has to be backed if found dead ground somewhere this season. The only time he ran on grass last year he did best of those to race down the centre behind Goretski on soft ground at Hamilton, and his current rating of 38 is somewhat handy when compared to that off which he started his handicap career at two for Bill Watts (85). He showed good form on the sand over the winter, too, including when just touched off by 70-rated Pharoah's Gold, giving 1lb, at Southwell on 24 January.

BOANERGES (IRE)

He was unlucky with the draw on at least five occasions last season and, despite winning a valuable 5f handicap at Musselburgh, starts this season only 3lb higher, on 78. With any luck, he'd have won three or four, including the Ayr Silver Cup (in which he beat the stands'-side group easily off 81) and now be rated in the high 80s. At his happiest when held up off a fast pace on an easy course, races like the Great St Wilfrid and Stewards' Cup would seem ideal.

BRIMSTONE (IRE)

Lightly-raced and seemingly fragile, he surely has to win a fast-ground, low-grade (Class E or F) handicap this season if finally handed a draw. Noted staying on really well to do best of the stands'-side group behind Northern Svengali at Hamilton last June, he didn't look happy on softer going the next two runs, before splitting the interesting pair, Haulage Man and Windchill, at Newcastle on his final start. Backed down from 20-1 to single figures for Blessingindisguise's race at Newcastle on Pitmen's Derby day off the back of his Hamilton effort (only to be withdrawn at the start), he starts this year very fairly treated on 45.

CATCHTHEBATCH

Although his Turf rating has been put up 6lb in the close-season thanks to his success on the All-Weather (he's gone up over a stone on that surface) he remains fairly treated, and has to be followed when found good or good to soft ground somewhere. After a couple of quiet ones on his return from

13 months off, he caught they eye at Folkestone last August, finishing well clear up the unfavoured stands' rail and second overall. Probably unsuited by fast ground and downhill Goodwood on his following two Turf outings, he is very quick and has to be backed the first time he's drawn near a favoured rail on a flat, straight course (he doesn't look happy round a bend).

CELTIC BALLET

She made a meal of winning a Catterick nursery after her excellent Ascot run – beat the unfavoured stands'-side group by 4l+ in the valuable Sales race last September – but remains unexposed and open to any amount of improvement over middle-distances this season.

CHELSEA BLUE (ITY)

She starts this season on a very handy mark of 65 and remains completely unexposed after just six runs last year. Easily first home up the far side at Ripon last July – the stands' side were favoured that day thanks to weight of numbers – the only two capable of beating her on the opposite flank were Listed-class Jessica's Dream and Fantasy Believer. The Handicapper could easily have gone back and put her up more than 1lb for that, and her final start at Yarmouth can be ignored on account of a slipping saddle (drawn wrong in any case).

CONTACT

He starts this Turf season on his lowest-ever rating and will recoup the losses sooner or later. First noted as interesting when doing best of the low numbers in Halland Park Girl's Tattersalls Breeders' race at The Curragh for Jim Bolger (duly followed up over-turning an O'Brien hotpot), he showed little in his first three starts for Michael Wigham. Heavily punted at Newmarket on his fourth and final start of 2000, connections rather chose the wrong day as, despite beating his group easily to finish sixth, he had no chance from his draw (first six drawn 13, 17, 21, 22, 20 and 2 of 28). Again heavily supported at Wolverhampton, from 4-1 to 2-1 in December, he never looked entirely happy on the surface (and hasn't since); his day will come.

CUMBRIAN CRYSTAL

Described as tall and scopey ahead of her debut last year (when she showed immense promise from a draw in no-man's land at Ripon), she again caught the eye on her second and final start on heavy ground at Haydock, picking up well at the finish. Expect huge improvement this time round.

DANAKIM

He is basically a dodgepot, but he starts this season well handicapped on 50 (his sole win to date came off 54 at Ripon last July) thanks to being handed endless impossible tasks on ground slower than he prefers last backend. Seemingly a stone better horse at Beverley – third from stall 7 of 19 and a close-up sixth from 1 of 17 in four starts there (faced impossible tasks the other twice) – watch him go when he finally lands a draw in a fast-ground 5f handicap there. He showed real promise from a poor draw on his Musselburgh return.

DEVON DREAM (IRE)

He has solid handicap form to his name off much higher marks than his current 41, and is the sort with whom Milton Bradley excels. Raced predominately round tight, turning courses such as Brighton by his previous trainer, he showed his best form last season at Chepstow, finishing a close third from stall 4 of 19 over 7f16y on fast ground (would have won but for Gary Hind putting up 3lb over).

DOUBLE BREW

He will not inspire many with '01 form figures 34084060 coming into this season, but there are any amount of valid excuses hidden away in there. From left to right: 3rd – beaten off levels by horses who finished the year rated 90 and 114, 4th – beaten 0.75l in a Newmarket handicap, 0 – hampered in Ascot handicap won by Corridor Creeper, 8th – no obvious excuse but may have found the firm ground too fast, 4th – raced alone up the slower stands' side at Newmarket, 0 – raced in a small group down the middle at Goodwood on a day the stands' rail was easily best, 6th – an outlier at Newmarket (first six drawn 1, 2, 3, 9, 7 and 17 of 21), and 0 – didn't take to the All-Weather. He starts this year rated just 72 and Les Eyre will find the right openings.

FFYNNON GOLD

Although she'd already had nine runs at three, she still looked green at the start of last year; it was amazing she was able to win first time out having unshipped and bolted before the start at Southwell. A winner from a desperate draw at Windsor in July (racing widest of all from 3 of 17 on good to firm), she ran a cracker from an impossible starting position at Lingfield three runs later, easily beating the far-side group by the best part of 3l. Possibly over the top when brought back for two runs last autumn, she starts this season on 57, just 1lb higher than at Lingfield, and has to be watched if found fast ground for her comeback, especially if she's drawn next to a left-hand rail.

HAULAGE MAN

Described as weak at two when not looking to finish his races, he remains open to any amount of improvement and will land a good few 6f handicaps if his Newcastle win last September is any guide. Always widest out towards the centre that day from stall 13, he effectively beat his group by 6l+, with the action focussed towards the far rail. While some will feel that his handicap mark was damaged by Don Eddy choosing to race him from out of the handicap over 7f50y in a much better race at Ayr next time (ran off 64 having won off 48 and starts this season on 59), he could quite easily be a 70-80 horse.

KYLLACHY

He looked a potential superstar when winning from stall 1 of 14 at Sandown on his comeback, particularly given that he had to come round the entire field on soft ground (stalls far side). Although things didn't quite go to plan afterwards, he obviously goes well fresh and could be worth chancing if sent for something like the Temple Stakes first time out.

NIVERNAIS

A cheap buy as a yearling, he showed serious promise on all three runs last year when not once handed a draw. After showing up well for a long way from 5 of 14 on his debut at Windsor, he managed the near-impossible at Folkestone when beating a bigger group to race up the far rail from stall 6 of 16 over 5f on good ground (almost 3l back to the next one on his side). Again stuck wide on his final start at Chepstow (drawn 7 of 20), he was only beaten a short-head, rallying after still looking a touch green. That came off 74; he starts this year only 2lb higher.

ORANGINO

It is with mixed emotions that he's included in this section, having cost one of the authors a serious amount of cash when beaten over 7f at Haydock last June. However, apparently there was a valid excuse for that disappointment in that he returned with a problem (which he should now be over fully). After a couple of never-threatening runs at two, when in need of the experience, he caught the eye first time out last year, staying on late behind Banjo Bay at Pontefract, but it was his first handicap run which marked him down as a horse of potential. One of only a handful to come up the stands' rail in the race won by Some Will over 6f at Haydock, he was noted staying on powerfully at the end to pull 7l clear of his group without having a chance of winning outright. A quietly fancied 5-1 on his next start, injury stopped him, and he never seemed quite right afterwards, including when tried back at 5f and in blinkers. Well handicapped as a result, on a mark of 44, he has to be kept on the right side this year.

PERTEMPS FC

He starts this Turf season on a mark only 3lb higher than that off which he started last year, on 48, despite one win, several placed efforts and little luck with the draw (030492182788560). From left to right: 0 – missed the break, 3rd – missed the break (only beaten 1.75l), 0 – missed the break and crowded out from a high draw at Beverley, 4th – came too wide from a middle draw at Beverley, 9th – no excuse at Newcastle, 2nd – 'won' the stands'-side race at Haydock, 1st, 8th – not beaten far at Goodwood (a course that wouldn't be ideal), 2nd – beaten a short-head from stall 17 at Pontefract, 7th – drawn wrong at Redcar, 8th – drawn wrong at Musselburgh, 8th – no excuse at Musselburgh, other than that the course probably doesn't suit, 5th – from stall 8 on too-soft ground at Chester, 6th – from out of the handicap on good to soft at Newcastle, and 0 – heavy ground. Pay particular attention when he's handed fast ground and a stiff 5f at a course where a slow start won't cost him (as it has done at Beverley).

PIERPOINT (IRE)

He has done most of his racing in the last 18 months on the All-Weather (without much success) but is equally well treated on Turf now and showed more than once last June that he has further races in him. Traditionally at his best in the summer, his efforts to finish fifth from stall 2 of 19 at Beverley, third to the progressive My American Beauty at Pontefract and second over the too-sharp Ripon five within a fortnight, off 59, 59 and 58 (starts this year on 58) suggested he'll win one at least this time when the ground firms up as did his Warwick run from a wide draw on Easter Monday.

Premier Baron (in front) will win his usual one or two again, over 7f off a fast pace

PREMIER BARON

Perhaps one of the most reliable horses in training, he rarely fails to deliver when everything is in his favour and will again land one or two this time. Capable of winning off ratings of up to 80 and always of interest when dropping to 75 or lower, he needs a testing 7f (either a stiff course on ground up to good to firm or an easy track on softer going) and a fast pace.

RED CHARGER (IRE)

Rated as high as 87 for Alan Berry at two, he starts this season on just 46 and will be worth backing if found soft ground somewhere (possibly with the blinkers back on). Only returned to action in October last year, he showed his best form in ages when finishing first of the stands'-side group and sixth overall on heavy ground behind Taras Emperor at Ayr (first six drawn 11, 3, 8, 4, 5 and 20 of 18) second time back. His subsequent unplaced run from an impossible draw on the Fibresand at Southwell can be ignored.

RIDICULE

Form figures of 0940 aren't going to excite many, but he's going to be a much better horse this year, and all those defeats were excusable anyway. Described as scopey ahead of his debut at Thirsk (where he was drawn on the wrong side and missed the break), he had no chance back at the same course second time after getting squeezed out at the start. Although well beaten by Captain Rio at Ripon on his penultimate outing, he did best of those to race up the stands' rail, and his final run at Nottingham can be ignored on account of racing up the stands' rail (with one other, Merely A Monarch, who won his next race).

SALVIATI (USA)

Trained by Amanda Perrett at three, he had a typical Milton Bradley season last year, running himself into form after four starts and then performing consistently well, often in the face of difficult draws or conditions. Only beaten by Cold Climate (who was at the top of his game at the time) on his fifth start, his next run really caught the eye, with him comfortably beating the stands'-side group (including Brevity) in Undeterred's race at Newcastle. Unlucky to be done by Juwwi's late finish at York, he went on to win at Ascot and Bath (ran well from an impossible draw at Beverley in between) before looking over the top in the Portland. He starts this season on a fair mark of 86 and connections now know he's best ridden allowed to use his high cruising speed over 5f or an easy 6f.

SIR DON (IRE)

After a promising debut when sent off 12-1 behind two previous winners, he caught everyone's eye at Thirsk second time, when easily beating the group to race towards the far side by 10l+ (first six drawn 11, 5, 16, 9, 13 and 10). Although slightly disappointing when turned over at odds-on on his final start (money for one of Eustace's is often a good guide), he remains very interesting.

SOTONIAN (HOL)

Although an infrequent winner on Turf, he showed himself as good as ever last summer, running an incredible race down the centre over 5f at Beverley (2nd of 17 from stall 4) and duly winning next time off a 2lb higher mark at Catterick (his second win there). The Yorkshire air obviously suit him (he's run well from moderate draws many times in the past two seasons at Beverley) and he should be watched if sent there, or back to Catterick, on good or faster ground when rated 55 or lower.

SPEEDY JAMES (IRE)

Listed class at two and three, he hasn't won for four years but is well weighted now on 55 after showing promise in a couple of soft-ground handicaps last backend. After giving signs of a comeback behind Fearby Cross at Doncaster last September, he went on to do best of the stands'-side group in Sharp Hat's race at Newcastle (by 2l) and is one to watch for whenever the rain arrives. A couple of pathetic efforts on the All-Weather in January can only help his price first time.

TEYAAR

Very well handicapped now on Turf, he's run well from a bad draw on more than one occasion in the past two seasons and invariably starts a campaign on a fair mark as a result of losing his way in the autumn. Happiest when allowed plenty of daylight, watch for him when he's drawn top or bottom of the shop over 6f on good or softer ground.

THUNDERCLAP

He could well be up to winning a decent early 7f handicap off a mark of 80, given that he remains unexposed after five runs (including one on the All-Weather at Lingfield, where he didn't handle the course). Drawn on the wrong side at Ripon on his second start after a promising debut (when in need of the run), he was again drawn down the wrong side in the big sales race at Doncaster after winning a tinpot Brighton maiden.

THUMAMAH (IRE)

She starts this season on a mark of 65 – a rating that represents sheer guesswork on the part of the Handicapper, as she had no chance from her draw on any of her three outings at two. A scopey half-sister to 90-rated 7f handicapper Rayyaan, she was sent off 9-4 favourite for her debut at Goodwood, having been the subject of good reports beforehand, but blew any chance she may have had by being brought to race alone up the slower stands' rail. Although only eighth on her second start, she did best of those to race down the centre at Kempton, in a race dominated by high numbers, and on her final start she was always widest out on firm ground at Pontefract in a race run in course-record time. Expect massive improvement this year.

TOMMY SMITH

Nominated by John Balding as this year's potential Beyond The Clouds after he'd won at Beverley last August, he's very fast and must be watched if going back there and landing a high draw. Although a winner at the course only once in several visits, he's had valid excuses for the defeats, including when twice running well from a bad draw (behind Leaping Charlie when never near the rail from 12 of 17, and when a close-up fourth to Madies Pride from 9 of 20 – his best effort to date). Occasionally inclined to boil over and play up at the stalls, don't be surprised to see him end up rated in the 80s (now 68) come the end of the year. Ignore his comeback run down the middle at Musselburgh

WINDCHILL

The winner of two sellers as a juvenile, she rarely disappoints when faced with a straight, stiff 6f or easy 7f and fast ground. Best of those to race up the stands' side off a rating of 52 in General Hawk's 7f handicap at Newcastle last July (beating the progressive Scarrottoo on her side), she had excuses afterwards, including when third to Haulage Man and Brimstone on her final start (hit over the head by a whip). Not very big, a mark of 47 is likely to get her into low-grade handicaps off a low weight once the ground firms up.

SPRINTLINE TOP TEN

While all the 125 horses listed in this section will hopefully pay their way this year, some are obviously open to more improvement than others. Here are the ten we consider most likely to go on to comparative greatness:

CUMBRIAN CRYSTAL

HAULAGE MAN

INDIAN BAZAAR

NIVERNAIS

ORANGINO

RIDICULE

SALVIATI

SOBA JONES

THUMAMAH

TOMMY SMITH

JOCKEYS TO FOLLOW

The following jockeys have either shown draw knowledge above and beyond the call of duty in the past, or successfully went against the crowd last year (in which case ('01) appears after their name (watch for them when they're drawn top or bottom of the shop and have the option of switching to a potentially favoured rail)):

G.Baker	('01, Race 5519, stayed centre at Windsor)
G.Carter	(very good)
A.Culhane	(always prepared to try something different)
K.Darley	
T.Durcan	
K.Fallon	(though not as good positional sense last year)
M.Fenton	
P.Fessey	
J.Fortune	
Helen Garrett	('01, Race 4189, stayed far side at Musselburgh)
D.Gibson	
G.Hannon	('01, Race 3680, went alone to far side at Windsor).
G.Hind	
R.Hughes	(very good)
D.Kinsella	('01, Race 5177, stayed centre at Windsor)
C.Lowther	
D.McKeown	
T.Quinn	
M.Roberts	(still the best and fingers crossed he recovers from injury)
J.Stack	
R.Winston	

INDEX

An alphabetical list of all horses in this section, along with their ideal conditions:

FFYNNON GOLD	6f, fast ground
FLAK JACKET	6f, June-August, recent run
FRIAR TUCK	6f, fast ground, small field
GDANSK (IRE)	5f, good to soft or softer ground, fresh
GENIAL GENIE	6f, good or faster ground
GET STUCK IN (IRE)	6f, G-S or softer ground, easy course
GOODENOUGH MOVER	7f, fast ground, straight course
GORETSKI (IRE)	5f, good to soft or softer ground, June-August
HARMONIC WAY	6f, fast ground, big field
HAULAGE MAN	6f, fast ground
HENRY HALL (IRE)	5f, good ground, Class C or lower
HILLTOP WARNING	7f, fast ground, fresh
INDIAN BAZAAR (IRE)	5f, fast ground, big field, recent run
INDIAN SPARK	5f, small field
JAWHARI	5f, fast ground or All-Weather, fresh
JUWWI	6f, fast ground, big field, recent run
KYLLACHY	5f, good or softer ground
LATE NIGHT OUT	7f, good or softer ground, turning course, fresh
LION'S DOMANE	7f, fast ground, turning course
LOVE'S DESIGN (IRE)	1m, fast ground, strong pace
MAMMAS F-C (IRE)	5f, fast ground, recent run
MARSAD (IRE)	6f, good or softer ground, fresh
MOUSEHOLE	5f, fast ground, June-August
MY BROTHER	6f, easy course, fresh
NIGRASINE	6f, fast ground, small field, Class C or lower
NIVERNAIS	yet to show his ideal conditions
NORTHERN SVENGALI (IRE)	5f, fast ground, Class E or lower, recent run
NOW LOOK HERE	6f, G-S- ground, outside Group class, fresh
ORANGINO	6f, good or faster ground
PANDJOJOE (IRE)	6f, fresh
PATRICIAN FOX (IRE)	5f, good or softer ground, fresh
PATSY CULSYTH	6f, good to soft or faster ground, fresh
PAYS D'AMOUR (IRE)	7f, fast ground, race worth under £10,000
PERTEMPS FC	5f, fast ground, stiff course
PETARGA	5f110y, Class D or lower, off for 7-20 days
PICCOLO CATIVO	6f, good to soft or softer ground, fresh
PIERPOINT (IRE)	5f, fast ground, stiff course
PLEASURE TIME	5f, fast ground, flat course, fresh
POP THE CORK	5f, fast ground, easy course
PREMIER BARON	7f, good ground, stiff course, fast pace
PRINCESS ALMORA	6f, good or faster ground, flat course, rail draw
PRIX STAR	6f, good to soft or faster ground, rail draw
PTARMIGAN RIDGE	5f, good or softer ground, fresh
RED CHARGER (IRE)	5f, soft or heavy ground, blinkers
REDOUBTABLE (USA)	6f, Classified Stakes
REGAL SONG (IRE)	5f, soft or heavy ground
RIDICULE	yet to show his ideal conditions
RITA'S ROCK APE	5f, fast ground, right-hand rail
ROSES OF SPRING	5f, fast ground, small field

RUSHCUTTER BAY	5f, Newmarket
RYEFIELD	6f, Ayr, recent run
SALVIATI (USA)	5f, good or faster ground
SAND HAWK	7f, G-S- ground (or Fibresand), recent run
SEVEN NO TRUMPS	6f, spring or autumn, Class B or below
SHARP HAT	5f, small field, recent run
SILKEN WINGS (IRE)	6f, fast ground, rail draw
SIR DESMOND	5f, flat course
SIR DON (IRE)	yet to show his ideal conditions
SMART PREDATOR	5f, good to soft or faster ground
SOAKED	5f, May-August, Class D or below, recent run
SOBA JONES	6f, not All-Weather, small field
SOTONIAN (HOL)	5f, good or good to firm ground
SPEEDY JAMES (IRE)	5f, good to soft or softer ground
SPENCERS WOOD (IRE)	6f, good to soft or softer ground
SUPERFRILLS	6f, draw within two of the rail
TALBOT AVENUE	5f, recent run
TARAS EMPEROR (IRE)	5f, heavy ground
TAYIF	6f, flat course, big field
TECHNICIAN (IRE)	6f, fast ground, recent run
TEYAAR	6f, good or softer ground
THAT MAN AGAIN	5f, fast ground, small field, right-hand rail
THE TRADER	5f, fast ground, blinkers
THUMAMAH (IRE)	yet to show her ideal conditions
THUNDERCLAP	yet to show his ideal conditions
TIME N TIME AGAIN	5f, fresh
TOMMY SMITH	5f, fast ground
VISION OF NIGHT	6f, fast ground, small field
VITA SPERICOLATA (IRE)	5f, fast ground, small field, race worth <£15k
WHO GOES THERE	7f, fast ground, straight course
WINDCHILL	7f, fast ground, low weight
ZUHAIR	5f, fast ground, easy course

NOTES

NOTES